CORNWALL

▲ St Just in Roseland

Produced jointly by the Publishing Division of
The Automobile Association and the Ordnance Survey

Editorial contributors: Rennie Bere (Wildlife); Dr V Challinor Davies (Gardens); David Clarke (Gazetteer; short features); Cornwall Archaeological Unit (The Ancient Landscape; The Industrial Landscape); Anne Duffin (Fighting Cornishmen); Des Hannigan (Gazetteer revisions for new edition; Long Distance Footpaths; Tours; Walks); Donald Rawe (Legends); Rebecca Snelling (Fact File)

Original photography: Andrew Lawson and Neil Ray

Typeset by Microset Graphics Ltd., Basingstoke, Hampshire
Colour separation by Daylight Colour Art Pte, Singapore
Printed and bound by
BPC PAULTON BOOKS LTD
A member of the British Printing Company Ltd.

Maps extracted or derived from the Ordnance Survey 1:625 000 Routeplanner Series, 1:250 000 Routemaster Series and 1:25 000 Pathfinder Series with the permission of Her Majesty's Stationery Office. Crown copyright.

Additions to the maps by the Cartographic Department of The Automobile Association and the Ordnance Survey.

Distributed in the United Kingdom by the Ordnance Survey, Southampton, and the Publishing Division of The Automobile Association, Norfolk House, Priestley Road,Basingstoke, Hampshire RG24 9NY. Registered number 1878835).

First edition 1987
Reprinted with amendments 1990
Revised edition 1992
Reprinted 1994

AA ISBN 0 7495 0371 8 (hardback)
AA ISBN 0 7495 0381 5 (softback)
OS ISBN 0 319 00292 6 (hardback)
OS ISBN 0 319 00283 7 (softback)

Introduction: Mousehole Harbour

Contents

▲ St Nectan's Pottery, Tintagel

Introduction

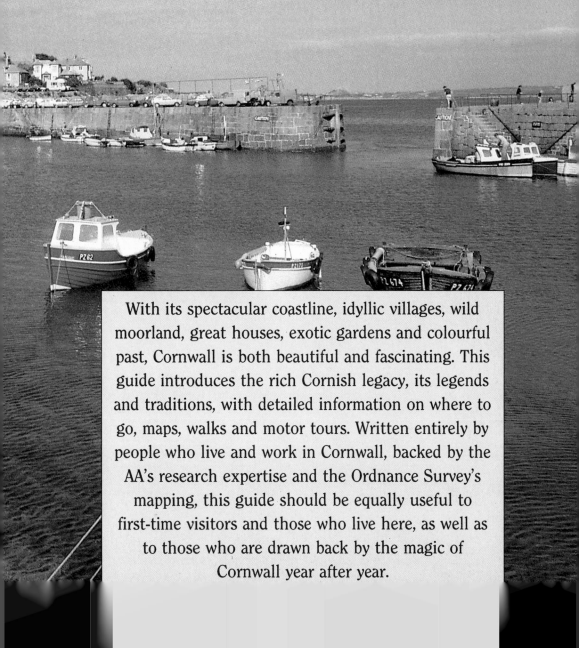

With its spectacular coastline, idyllic villages, wild moorland, great houses, exotic gardens and colourful past, Cornwall is both beautiful and fascinating. This guide introduces the rich Cornish legacy, its legends and traditions, with detailed information on where to go, maps, walks and motor tours. Written entirely by people who live and work in Cornwall, backed by the AA's research expertise and the Ordnance Survey's mapping, this guide should be equally useful to first-time visitors and those who live here, as well as to those who are drawn back by the magic of Cornwall year after year.

The Ancient Landscape

We are all used to peeping over a hedge to glimpse a ploughed-up Bronze Age burial mound standing in a field of broccoli or oil seed rape; finding a fragment of mediaeval wall or arched window amongst the modern shops; or being drawn to the gaunt and dramatic engine-houses that stand on scrub ground. It takes a leap of imagination to think of the barrow in its original gladed sacred setting, or to picture the bustle of the mediaeval town. It is

equally hard to imagine the acres of wooden, tin-roofed processing buildings clustered about a smoking engine-house, the air thick with smoke and fumes of sulphur and arsenic.

The landscape, too, has changed. The remains of prehistoric stone round houses and mediaeval farmsteads on the now bleak hillslopes of Bodmin Moor and Penwith require us to recognise these as once productive and pleasant places to live. Since late prehistory, much of the county had been uncultivated moorland, surviving largely intact until the late 18th century. Once widespread in Cornwall, the traditional farm holding of field and moor now survives only in Penwith and around Bodmin Moor. It is within the former moorlands that the most dramatic landscape changes have occurred through mining, china-clay extraction, quarrying and enclosure for farming.

Hunters and gatherers, 8,000–4,000BC.

At the close of the Ice Age, 10,000 years ago, the coast of Cornwall lay up to four miles further out than today. The ice melted, raising the sea level, gradually drowning the coastal lowlands. The climate warmed rapidly and vegetation changed from tundra through coniferous and finally to mixed oak woodland. Bands of nomads hunted red deer, ox and pig in the forest and gathered berries, nuts, and plants. In summer they hunted on the open uplands, following the animals into the lowland woods in the winter. In the spring and autumn they moved to the coast, rich in fish, shellfish and grey seals. Little is now left of this, the Mesolithic period, but scatters of flint implements.

Settlers and monument-builders, 4,000–2,500BC

By 4,000BC the idea of agriculture had spread, and areas of woodland were systematically cleared. Excavations have shown that over the next few thousand years settled communities drastically changed the appearance of the landscape. In Cornwall, on the rocky summits of Carn Brea near

Left: Iron Age village street at Chysauster
Right: the Mên-an-Tol stone, near Lanyon
Below left: the Hurlers, by the road just west of Minions. Tradition says they are men petrified for playing hurling on the Sabbath
Below right: aerial view of St Dennis, showing the Iron Age hill-fort in which the church stands

Camborne and Helman Tor, Lanlivery, massive stone ramparts were built around settlements of sub-rectangular houses. On the slopes below, plots were cleared for cultivation. At Carn Brea hundreds of flint arrowheads found in the excavations suggest that the settlement was sacked.

Little is known of where other people lived but Neolithic society was well-organised and capable of wide-ranging trade in Cornish stone axes, now found as far afield as Essex, and pottery made on the Lizard was distributed throughout the south-west. The great megalithic chamber tombs or quoits, a type common to the whole Atlantic seaboard, are well known. Built as expressions of religious belief and communal affiliation as much as repositories for the dead, they are mute evidence of the toil and skill required to erect them.

Farmers, ceremonial and burial monuments, 2,000–600BC

As the landscape filled up with the farms of round houses, sacred areas were set aside for many forms of ceremonial and burial monuments. Embanked ritual enclosures (with ditches on the inside) known as henges, as at Castilly, Bodmin, were succeeded by stone circles, standing stones (menhirs), and stone rows as important ritual monuments. Many are found in Cornwall, those on Bodmin Moor and Penwith being the best known. Around the Merry Maidens in Penwith is a fine example of a sacred area: several menhirs (the Pipers) and a cluster of burials surround the stone circle. One of these, Tregiffian, is an entrance grave: a Bronze Age development of Neolithic quoits, common in

Aerial view of Zennor, showing clearly the irregular pattern of the stone walls built on top of the original prehistoric field boundaries

Penwith and Scilly. Elsewhere, sacred areas contain cemeteries of burial mounds (barrows or stone cairns, marked tumuli on maps) erected over the cremated remains of prominent individuals. Several such cemeteries are visible, particularly those at Four Burrows and Carland Cross on the A30 north of Truro.

Surrounding them were farmland, pasture and settlements, now invisible in lowland Cornwall. It is on Bodmin Moor and in Penwith that Bronze Age landscapes can best be appreciated. Here on now bleak moorland stood hundreds of thatched stone round houses occupied at a time when the weather was some two degrees Centigrade warmer than today and soils were more fertile. On Bodmin Moor on the slopes of Roughtor and on the surrounding hills, over 500 ruined houses have been found with their associated stone-banked fields and nearby burial cairns and stone circles. Heaps of cleared stone and soil build-up (lynchets) against the lower edges of the fields are evidence of the cultivation that once took place. The farmers with their simple scratch ploughs would have been constantly reminded of their ancestors by the cairns that crown the hilltops and ridges all around. Below, in the more wooded valleys, lay deposits of tin gravel probably exploited at this early date to make, with copper, the bronze for tools, weapons and jewellery. Gold from further afield was beaten into armlets and neck pieces.

Hill-forts and the Celts, 600BC–AD43
The dominant monuments of the Iron Age are the hill-forts. Cornwall has an extraordinary number

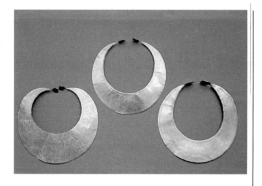

The gold collars, dating from about 1800BC, found at Harlyn Bay and (centre) St Juliot

and variety of defended sites. Even in decay their tumbled ramparts and silted ditches are impressive. Some have multiple defences with complicated entrances, others known as cliff-castles have huge ramparts thrown across narrow-necked coastal promontories (eg The Rumps, Pentire Head). These were the strongholds of the warrior aristocracy and the centres of tribal power from which they exacted tribute and directed trade.

Surrounding them were the smaller but nonetheless defended rounds: enclosed by a single bank and ditch they were probably the homes of freemen. Both these and other unenclosed farms sat amongst extensive fields that in Penwith have proved so durable that their form and layout still survives; in Zennor the stone walls defining small irregular fields lie on top of the original prehistoric field boundaries.

Also amongst the fields are courtyard houses: dwellings and farm buildings opening on to an unroofed courtyard. Chysauster is a village of over ten such houses arranged along a street. Carn Euny has, like many sites on the Atlantic seaboard, a fogou: an underground passage, presumably used for storage or ritual.

The Romans, AD43–410
Following the Claudian invasion of AD43, Vespasian with the second Augustan Legion marched west. By the mid-50s, the provincial capital Isca Dumnoniorum (Exeter) was founded to control the main territory of the Dumnonii, the Celtic tribe of Cornwall, Devon and West Somerset. The only known fort in Cornwall, at Nanstallon, Bodmin, housed a mixed 500-man auxiliary detachment of infantry and cavalry. The native strongholds were abandoned, and in the countryside life continued much as before in the rounds and courtyard houses. The enormous market of the Roman Empire widened trading opportunities, although tin was not at first in great demand as sources elsewhere were used. Fine tableware was imported to Cornwall from eastern Britain, the Continent and the Mediterranean, and coinage introduced.

The uplands, abandoned around 1,000BC because of deteriorating climate, were not reoccupied. The already developing farms in the lowlands helped to feed an expanding rural population. Towards the end of the period, early farms were abandoned and new hamlets established, and it is this pattern of settlements which survives to this day.

Cornwall appears to have been an isolated corner of the westernmost extremity of the Empire, still essentially Celtic in character and religion.

The Age of Saints and the kingdom of Cornwall, AD410–1066

The Celtic aristocracy was now free to rule and a network of independent kingdoms re-emerged over the British Isles. Cornwall was part of the kingdom of Dumnonia. The names of some rulers may be recorded on the inscribed memorial stones which dot the Cornish countryside. Their seats were re-fortified, defended sites, the most spectacular and renowned of which was Tintagel where excavations have revealed the trappings of a royal household.

Independence was short-lived, for by the 8th century the English had reached the Tamar, and by the 10th had nominal control of Cornwall. Dumgarth, drowned in 875, is the last Cornish king to be recorded; the Doniert Stone, St Cleer, may be his memorial. Although some rounds were inhabited until the 6th or 7th centuries, there was a gradual shift to unenclosed hamlets called trefs which by 1066 were the dominant settlement type: a move from stock-rearing to arable may be the reason. House styles were also changing: the earliest post-Roman buildings were round or oval, but at the 10th-century village of Mawgan Porth, rectangular houses were grouped around a courtyard.

Many farmers were also fishermen or tinners. The presence of Mediterranean pottery and continental influences on local styles suggests continuing trade with the Mediterranean, replaced by links with the Low Countries by the 9th century.

Christianity introduced from the Mediterranean and Wales brought fundamental changes. Nonetheless, ancient beliefs in the supernatural powers of springs lingered, and such sites were adopted as holy wells. Inscribed stones, commemorating important people, were set up beside tracks and fords, as well as in churchyards. Some have inscriptions in Ogham, the Irish stroke-alphabet, indicating the influence of Irish settlers in the spread of Christianity in Cornwall. True cross-carving began in the 9th century. The decorated crosses at St Neot, Cardinham, Sancreed and Lanherne are amongst the earliest and finest.

The 15th-century holy well at St Cleer was believed to be a healing well

Restormel Castle, mostly late 13th-century, a prime example of military architecture

Castles and hamlets, church and trade, AD1066–1540

After the Norman Conquest the new aristocracy stamped its authority on the Cornish with a formidable series of castles: Launceston and Trematon being strongholds of Robert of Mortain, who held most of the Cornish manors. Other castles belonged to his chief sub-tenants, as at Restormel and Cardinham. By the 13th century the major castles all belonged to the Earls of Cornwall, and their subsequent history was of neglect, as the absentee earls and dukes resided in Wallingford, Berkhamsted and Kennington, supported by the income from their Cornish estates.

The predominant settlement pattern was of single farms and small hamlets, surrounded by their open fields, divided into strips by low banks. The Forrabury Stitches at Boscastle give some idea of how large areas of Cornwall must have appeared.

Most parishes and parish churches are mediaeval in origin, and many are on sites that had been in use for worship since the 5th or 6th centuries. Churches form Cornwall's largest reserve of mediaeval buildings. Most manors of any pretension had a domestic chapel, as at Cotehele. Other chapels stood at bridges and fords, or doubled as lighthouses and daymarks; some served Cornwall's many leper hospitals. Few of these sites survive. The most obvious and enduring monuments to mediaeval piety are the hundreds of granite crosses that marked the paths to churches.

By the 14th century no-one in the county would have been more than six miles from a market. Cornwall had many small towns, some of them little more than villages. Many were fishing ports. Seaports traded with Brittany, Wales, Ireland and Spain, often mixing trade with piracy and smuggling. Some of the coastal towns suffered at the hands of French and Spanish raiders: Fowey (1457), Marazion (1514), Mousehole, Newlyn and Penzance (1595). Block-houses and batteries were built in the 15th and 16th centuries to counter this and the threat of invasion; most notably Henry VIII's artillery forts at Pendennis, St Mawes and St Catherine's Castle, Fowey.

Compared to most counties, Cornwall had a particularly diverse economy which gave it a special character then as in later centuries. Most people worked the land but thousands more were involved in the tin industry or in quarrying slate or granite, while others fished, or worked in lively seaports where the Cornish language, still dominant in the west of the county, might be heard amid the cosmopolitan hubbub of Breton and French, Spanish and English.

The Industrial Landscape

Cornwall's landscape is scarred with the traces of both ancient and modern mineral extraction. The majority of the more obvious industrial remains belong to the last two centuries, but during the previous 4,000 years tin played an important part in the economy of the county. During prehistory, tin was dug from valley gravels and smelted in primitive bowl furnaces to produce metal ingots (some are in the County Museum, Truro). Tin at this time was mainly alloyed with copper to produce bronze, and from this implements, jewellery and weaponry were made. Evidence for prehistoric tinworks comes largely from finds recovered in abandoned streamworks reworked during the 19th century, which revealed numerous artefacts.

In the early years of the Roman period, the major source of tin for the Empire was the deposits in north-western Spain and Cornish tin was little exploited. However, in the 3rd century AD the gradual exhaustion of these sources led to the re-working of many Cornish streamworks. Unfortunately, no known Roman or earlier tinworks survive today, and the earliest visible remains probably date to the mediaeval period.

Documentary and archaeological work show the importance to the mediaeval economy of the tin industry and some of the earthworks in the valley bottoms (particularly on Bodmin Moor) date to this period. The tinners were tightly controlled by the Stannary Courts, which laid down laws, and upheld the privileges of those involved in the industry. Generally, tinners were exempt from manorial services and taxes, but in return, the tin which they produced was very heavily taxed at the nearest coinage town (Liskeard, Bodmin, Lostwithiel,

Main picture: mid-19th-century engraving of Botallack mine. Right: engine-house remains are a common feature of the Cornish landscape. Below left: the last rotative beam-winding engine in Cornwall at East Pool. Below right: tin-miner's helmet, an exhibit in Zennor's museum

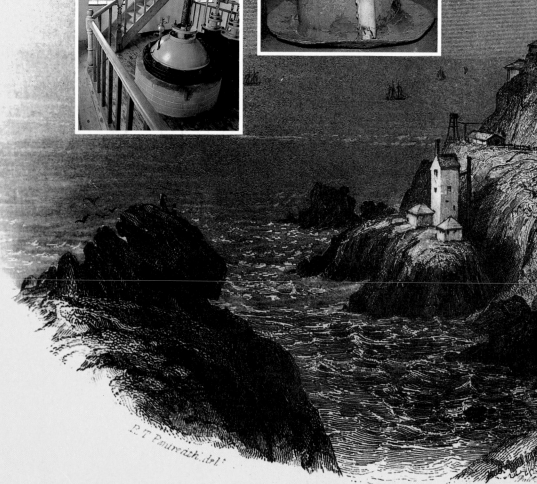

Truro and Helston). Throughout this period, technology developed rapidly, with mining of the ore by opencast quarries and shallow shafts being introduced from the late 13th century. Before the tin ore could be smelted, it was necessary to separate the cassiterite (tin oxide) from unwanted minerals, and this was achieved by crushing and grinding the ore in water-powered stamping and crazing mills. It was then concentrated and smelted in blast-furnaces known as blowing-houses. The remains of these structures are still visible, although many hundreds have been destroyed by later mining. The tin was cast into large rectangular ingots, and then taken to be 'coigned' (taxed) and sold. Much of it was taken by sea to London where the majority was used in the production of pewter, but significant amounts were also used to make church bells, solder, artillery and bronze construction machinery.

The Cornish Industrial Revolution

The visitor to Cornwall cannot help but notice the remains of mine engine-houses in the landscape. They are found from the east of the county in the Tamar Valley and on the southern slopes of Bodmin Moor, through the area around Camborne–Redruth and on the cliffs of St Agnes to the clifftop stacks to the far west of Penwith. These are the relics of an industry which in the late 18th and for much of the 19th centuries made the

county one of the foremost tin and copper producers in the world, a major centre of invention and engineering during the Industrial Revolution. The development of transport networks was encouraged, and wealth was created that financed both the growth of the modern urban centres and the creation of many small mining villages in areas formerly moorland or heath. Ports often developed into important industrial centres in their own right, Hayle having at one time two of the largest iron foundries in the county, while Calstock grew beside the Tamar to serve the needs of the busy mining area to the west.

The surviving engine-houses and the acres of spoil and derelict buildings which now surround them represent only a small part of enterprises whose chief remains now lie abandoned deep underground, or which consisted of structures of an extensive but temporary nature – these have now been swept away but can be seen in abundance on photographs of the period.

The onset of the Industrial Revolution had demanded increasing supplies, not only of iron and coal, but also of tin and copper; two essential raw materials for engineering which Cornwall was able, almost uniquely in Britain, to supply. It was the local development of the steam engine which allowed extraction in the quantities demanded and from depths previously impossible to drain using earlier technologies.

Publ. by H. Besley Directory Office South St. Exeter.

The first beam engine was erected in Cornwall in about 1716 and despite the almost prohibitive cost of transporting coal from South Wales, in all nearly 1,000 engines were eventually installed to pump water, haul ore from workings up to 3,000ft deep, and drive machinery to crush and refine the ore. A large number of these engines was built in world-famous foundries like Harvey's of Hayle or Perran Foundry, which also supplied anything from a 50ft waterwheel to a miner's shovel. Gunpowder mills like the Kennal works at Ponsanooth, National Explosives at Hayle Towans and Bickfords Fuse Works at Tuckingmill and other manufacturers supplied all local demand from candles and clothing to gasholders and drain covers. The huge demand for steam coal and timber, and the massive tonnage of copper ore to be sent to Wales for smelting, spurred the development of industrial harbours linked to the mines by railways. Nationally famous inventors and engineers like Newcomen, Smeaton, Trevithick, Davey and Murdoch emerged as industrial expertise developed, gained at first hand in the mines, foundries and engineering works of the area.

The history of first copper and then tin mining in the period 1820-1890 was marked by both booms and slumps, and although always a dangerous undertaking for the miners themselves and a gamble for the adventurers who put up the capital and pocketed the profits, mining was the basis for the economic prosperity of the county.

Fortunes were made and lost virtually overnight: employment on copper mines in 1837 was around 30,000; from 1866 to 1874, Cornish copper mining collapsed after discoveries were made of vast deposits in Chile and Australia. Over 12,000 miners emigrated, and it was said that at the bottom of a mine anywhere in the world one could find a Cornishman working. In 1870 there were 300 tin mines at work in the county; by 1896 cheaper tin from Bolivia and Malaya had forced the abandonment of all but a handful. A brief world demand for arsenic staved off the end for a while, but by the turn of the century it was virtually all over, and areas that had been intensively worked for centuries were finally abandoned. In 1986 only three tin mines remained at work.

Top: spectacular landscape for drivers on the road which passes the china-clay mine at Stannon Downs
Above: the engineer Richard Trevithick holds a model of his locomotive

China-clay

China-clay extraction has the most obvious and spectacular impact on the landscape. First discovered by William Cookworthy in 1746, china-clay was originally used with china-stone for making fine porcelain, but nowadays is also used in paper-making, chemicals and other industries. The main centre of extraction lies within the Hensbarrow granite uplands north of St Austell, with smaller areas in Penwith, on Tregonning Hill near Helston and on Bodmin Moor. Two centuries of active working have changed the moorland landscape to one of sheer-sided quarries and water-filled pits, surrounded by the white dumps of waste mica and quartz sand. China-clay is formed by the decomposition of feldspar within the granite to a chalky powder: this is extracted by washing the working face with a powerful jet of water, and settling the clay from the stream in large pits or tanks. Originally the clay was dried naturally in large, open-sided sheds, but in the 1850s the pan kiln was introduced to speed the process. These long low buildings with a tall chimney at one end are still a distinctive feature of the area, although they have now been superseded by modern driers. Transport of the clay was mostly seaborne and ports which grew up to serve this need at Par, Fowey and Charlestown are still in active use, whilst that at Pentewan is disused. The Wheal Martyn Museum at St Austell displays the history and technology of the industry in a preserved works of the 1880s.

A landscape of stone: Quarrying

Stone-working has for centuries been part of the county's economy and in many areas quarry villages have grown up around the workings. The availability of a wide variety of stone and suitable materials for brickmaking ensured virtual self-sufficiency in building materials until recently, and the slate from the North Cornish quarries, many perched precariously on the cliff-faces, roofed most of the buildings of the county.

Not all stone was cut from quarries: most granite uplands are pockmarked with small surface workings where boulders and outcrops have been split into blocks for gateposts, millstones, crosses, quoins and mullions. Crushed stone used for road and railway building is traditionally the hard elvan stone, produced at Penlee and Dean Quarries. Dimension or shaped stone was used for building, for cobbles, kerbstones, gravestones and building ornament. Pentewan, Cataclews and Polyphant stone as well as granite were all used in Cornish churches from an early period. Serpentine and soapstone from the Lizard, although briefly tried as a source of pottery clay, were used for their varied colours. The larger granite quarries had cranes, tramways, dressing sheds and blacksmiths' shops for making and sharpening tools. Working methods have developed from wood wedges to tar and feathers, from gunpowder to high explosives and thermic lances.

Transport

Throughout the mediaeval period and into the 18th century most goods were moved by packhorse and donkey. Cornish roads were in many cases too rutted and narrow for carts, severely hampering the development of local industry, and the sea continued to be used for the despatch of goods and by long-distance travellers. But many of the navigable estuaries which had been important in the mediaeval and earlier periods became so choked with tinners' waste that important ports such as Helston, Tregony and Lostwithiel were left stranded far above navigable limits. Penryn, once the pre-eminent port on the Fal, was rapidly eclipsed once Sir John Killigrew, Governor of Pendennis Castle, had built the

Above: the slate quarry at Delabole has been in production for almost six hundred years
Inset: Brunel's Royal Albert Bridge takes the railway across the Tamar at Saltash

settlement of Pennycomequick, now Falmouth. Falmouth Haven, one of the world's great deep-water anchorages became a major naval station and packet port for the Americas. In the early 19th century Padstow became one of the largest embarkation ports for emigrant miners. Most of the ports and many of the tidal inlets once had flourishing shipyards building coastal traders, in part to serve the 300 or more lime-kilns used for agricultural fertiliser. Fishing boats, pilot gigs, river craft and larger ocean-going vessels continued to be built until after the First World War even in obscure places like Calstock, Portmellion, St Columb Porth and Gweek.

Turnpike trusts were set up in the late 18th century and improved major roads, but had little impact on the development of industry, although stagecoaches could now provide a reliable, although expensive, service to London. Several short canals were laid out to serve specific needs, but the hilly terrain was unsuited to major works of this kind; it was the advent of railways which allowed Cornwall's mining industry to expand to its 19th-century peak. From 1809 onwards, many tramroads and railways were built to serve industry and the local community. These were at first entirely independent and isolated within Cornwall, until the main line from London was finally opened to Truro in 1859, carried across the Tamar by Brunel's Royal Albert Bridge. However, the Cornwall Railway's adoption of the broad gauge effectively prolonged the county's isolation from through-communication with northern Britain until the gauge conversion in 1892. By this time, the heyday of Cornish mining and industry was over – the mineral tramways and harbours had carried the bulk of the traffic. The main line finally came into its own when tourists began arriving in large numbers, but this role was to be short-lived; the laying of the first tarmacadam on the A30 in 1919 heralded a new age of motorised road transport and a new era for Cornwall.

Above: the north front of Antony House, home of the Carew family. Left: portrait of the historian of Cornwall, Sir Richard Carew

Fighting Cornishmen

Richard Carew, the Cornish historian, wrote of his fellow Cornish gentlemen in 1602 that '*They keepe liberall, but not costly builded or furnished houses, give kind entertainment to strangers, make even at the yeeres end with the profits of their living, are reverenced and beloved of their neighbours, live void of factions amongst themselves (at leastwise such as breake out into anie daungerous excesse) and delight not in braverie of apparrell; yet the woman would be verie loth to come behind the fashion, in newfanglednes of the maner, if not in costlynes of the matter, which perhaps might over-empty their husbands purses. They converse familiarly together, and often visit one another. A Gentleman and his wife will ride to make merry with his next neighbour; and after a day or twayne, those two couples goe to a third; in which progresse they encrease like snowballs, till through their burdensome waight they breake againe.*'

Like other notable members of the Cornish gentry, Richard Carew's grandsons, Sir Alexander and John Carew, lived and died amidst great drama. Sir Alexander Carew was beheaded in London in December 1644 for plotting to deliver St Nicholas Island at Plymouth to the Royalist enemy; whilst in contrast, his brother John Carew was one of the judges who tried King Charles I, and was executed as a regicide at the Restoration in 1660. Their home, Antony House, in Carew hands from the 15th century, now belongs to the National Trust.

Also in eastern Cornwall are the houses of Mount Edgcumbe and Cotehele, both formerly properties of the Edgcumbe family; Mount Edgcumbe, still occupied by the family, is open to the public, and Cotehele belongs to the National Trust. Carew relates how in 1483, the Lancastrian Richard Edgcumbe was being pursued by the Yorkist Henry Bodrugan, and hid in the woods at Cotehele, overlooking the Tamar, '*which extremity taught him a sudden policy, to put a stone in his cap and tumble the same into the water, while these rangers were fast at his heels, who looking down after the noise and seeing his cap swiming thereon, supposed that he had desperately drowned himself, gave over their further hunting and left him liberty to shift away and ship over into Brittany*', from which place he soon returned with Henry Tudor.

When Henry Tudor was crowned King Henry VII, after defeating Richard III, Richard Edgcumbe became powerful as one of the chief executors of crown policy. In February 1487 he was granted a commission to arrest Bodrugan and other Yorkist rebels 'who have withdrawn themselves into private places in the counties of Devon and Cornwall and stir up sedition'. The story goes that upon Edgcumbe's approach, Bodrugan slipped out of his house at Chapel Point near Mevagissey, leapt off the nearby cliffs and landed on a little grassy island 100ft below, where a boat was waiting to take him to a ship for France. The place is still known as Bodrugan's Leap.

In a later chapter in the history of the Edgcumbe family, after Sir Thomas Fairfax had led the Parliamentary forces across the Tamar in 1646, Colonel Pierce Edgcumbe conspired with some of his neighbours to surrender eastern Cornwall on advantageous terms, thus leaving the rest of the county open to the Parliamentarians and perhaps bringing about the ultimate collapse of the Royalist cause.

A sprightly gentleman

North of the Edgcumbe houses is Stow, one-time home of the Grenvile family, which has produced several Cornish heroes. Sir Richard Grenvile of the *Revenge* will always be remembered for his Elizabethan maritime successes, whilst his grandsons Sir Bevill and Sir Richard, were stalwart Royalists during the Civil War. Edward, Earl of Clarendon, historian of the Civil Wars, described Sir Bevill Grenvile as 'a gallant and sprightly gentleman, of the greatest reputation and interest in Cornwall' who was 'the generally most loved man of that county'. Sir Bevill has come to epitomise the Royalist cause in Cornwall, and inspired the poet Rev Robert Stephen Hawker to write:

. . . Call the hind from the plough, and the herd from
*   the fold,*
Bid the wassailer cease from his revel;
And ride for old Stow, where the banner's unrolled
For the cause of King Charles and Sir Bevill. . . .

At Braddock Down, near Boconnoc, a monument marks the site of the battle of January 1643 where, in a wild charge, Sir Bevill Grenvile led his servants and tenants down one hill and up another, so that they 'strook a terror' into the enemy. In May 1643, Sir Bevill and his fellow Cornish officers led their troops to another momentous victory at Stratton, near the Grenvile home at Stow. According to Clarendon, this 'seasonable victory' was celebrated by Sir Bevill Grenvile and Sir Ralph Hopton with 'public prayers upon the place and a solemn thanksgiving to Almighty God for their deliverance' and because of their success against the odds, Hopton is said to have declared that 'in the fight God blessed the King's party'.

Rebels across the Tamar

A plaque in Bodmin celebrates Thomas Flamank, a lawyer of the town. In 1497, a year of economic depression, Flamank and Michael Joseph, a blacksmith from the Lizard area, led 15,000

Mount Edgcumbe, near Torpoint, is still occupied by the Edgcumbe family

Plaque commemorating rebel-leaders Joseph and Flamank

Cornishmen to London to protest at being taxed to pay for a remote Scottish war. But the disillusioned and much-deserted Cornish force stood little chance of success against King Henry's 25,000 strong army at Blackheath on 16 June 1497. About 200 Cornishmen were killed in the ensuing battle, and both Flamank and Joseph were hanged, drawn, and quartered at Tyburn. This episode merely served to exacerbate anti-government feeling, so that the county proved to be an ideal springboard for Perkin Warbeck's claim, three months after the event, to be one of the Princes in the Tower who had not been murdered after all. Warbeck received a rapturous welcome in Cornwall, and in Bodmin was joined by some of the lesser gentry and proclaimed King Richard IV. He crossed the Tamar in September 1497 with 6,000 Cornish supporters, but they got no further than Taunton, where they were forced to surrender to the king.

In 1549, Bodmin again proved to be the natural centre of Cornish resistance to unpopular government measures. A full-scale rebellion broke out in reaction to the 1549 Act of Uniformity, with its enforcement of the Book of Common Prayer and its simplified service in English, in place of the old Latin mass. One of the complaints of the Cornishmen was that they could not understand

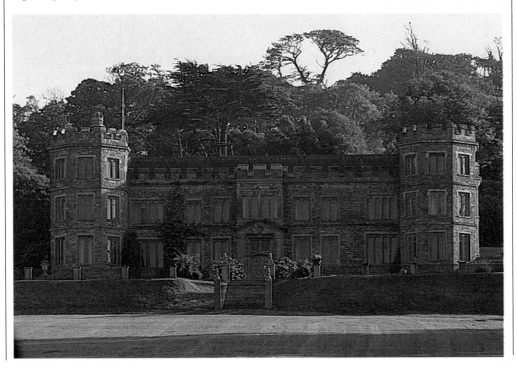

the new Prayer Book, 'and so we Cornishmen, whereof certain of us understand no English, utterly refuse thise new English'. Yet again an 'army' of Cornishmen marched from Bodmin across the Tamar, but with no more success than on previous occasions: they were routed by Henry VIII's troops in Devon, and their leaders executed. A century later, during the English Civil War, Bodmin maintained the same neutral stance as other Cornish towns, and entertained both Royalist and Parliamentarian officers in turn. However, in 1660-1661, the Mayors' Accounts record considerable expenditure on beer, buns, wine and bonfires in the streets, to celebrate the restoration and coronation of King Charles II. Not far from the town is Lanhydrock House, one-time home of the Robartes family, who through trade experienced a rapid rise in fortune and status in the early 17th century; by the mid-17th century Lord Robartes was one of the leaders of the Parliamentarian cause in Cornwall. Lanhydrock, more recently rebuilt after fire, is known as 'the grand old lady of Cornish houses', and is a National Trust property.

An honourable defeat

One of the ringleaders of the 1549 Prayer Book Rebellion was Humphry Arundel, a member of the oldest and most fanatically Catholic branch of the Arundel family. Humphry Arundel was executed for his actions, but the family maintained its faith, and partly because of this supported Charles I in 1642. Another branch of this family lived at Trerice Manor, eight miles south of Lanherne and three miles from Newquay. Sir John Arundell of Trerice, a staunch Royalist, was governor of Pendennis Castle, Falmouth, during the five-month siege of 1646. On 17 March 1646, Sir Thomas Fairfax occupied Arwenack Manor in Falmouth and ordered Arundell to surrender, only to receive this gallant reply: '. . . *having taken less than two minutes resolution, I resolve that I will here bury myself before I deliver up this Castle to such as fight against his Majesty*'. Eventually the garrison was starved into submission, but the Royalists maintained their dignity by making a surrender on honourable terms, and marched out of the castle

Above: memorial in Truro Cathedral to John Robartes, a leading Parliamentarian
Main picture: St Michael's Mount, centre of some turbulent episodes in history

with 'Drums beating, Colours flying, Trumpets sounding'. Pendennis Castle is open to the public; Trerice is a superb 16th-century manor house and belongs to the National Trust; Arwenack Manor is now private flats.

Falmouth harbour is overlooked on the other side by St Mawes Castle, which also supported the

Top: Pendennis Castle, the last Royalist stronghold in England to fall.
Bottom: St Mawes Castle also supported the Royalist cause

Royalist war effort in Cornwall, although it surrendered before Pendennis and without a fight. Sir Richard Vyvyan of Trelowarren suffered great financial loss by erecting another fort at Dennis Head in 1643-1644, at his own expense, to defend the Helford River for the king. Trelowarren has been the home of the Vyvyans since the 15th century. Sir Francis Godolphin of Godolphin House, near Helston, took up arms for King Charles I in 1642, and was governor of the Isles of Scilly; his younger brother, Sidney, the poet, was killed in the king's service at Chagford in 1643. His death was a major blow to his friends and contemporaries, Sir Bevill Grenvile writing to his wife that he *'was a gallant a gent as the world had'*, whilst Sir Ralph Hopton said he was *'as perfect and as absolute a piece of vertue as ever our nation bredd.'* Godolphin House is in private (though not Godolphin) hands, and is sometimes open.

Rebellion's back-door

Some of the most turbulent episodes surround St Michael's Mount off Cornwall's southern coast. In 1473, after the Yorkist Edward IV had been established on the throne, the rebel Earl of Oxford seized St Michael's Mount by disguising his men as pilgrims. He was besieged by successive Sheriffs of Cornwall: Sir John Arundell of Trerice (who was killed in a skirmish on the sands dividing the Mount from the mainland, thus fulfilling a prophecy to that effect), Sir Henry Bodrugan, and Richard Fortescue. The siege lasted four months, far longer than the king considered necessary; indeed, according to tradition, Edward attributed this to the disloyalty of the Cornish, and he thereafter regarded Cornwall as 'the back door of rebellion'. Between 1642 and 1646 the garrison at the Mount was held for the king by its owners, the Bassett family of Tehidy. Sir Arthur Bassett surrendered the Mount to Parliament in April 1646. During the Commonwealth, St Michael's Mount passed into the hands of John St Aubyn, who had supported Parliament during the war; his descendant, Lord St Levan, is living there today.

Legends

As a land of legend Cornwall is difficult to surpass. Within its tiny area many hundreds of stories and myths have survived, some based on evident historical fact, others whose origins are lost in antiquity. Here is a fascinating field for the student of folklore.

The Cornish Giants and Fairy-Folk, or Piskies, are among the most notable of legends. The idea of the giants, it has been suggested, originated when the tall Celts arrived in Cornwall around 500BC. Being so much larger than the Neolithic and Bronze Age peoples before them, they were looked on as giants; conversely the Celts regarded their squat, dark predecessors as dwarfs or piskies.

Tales of the giants amused our ancestors down the ages, and were recorded mainly in West Cornwall. St Michael's Mount, that jewel of an island off Marazion, was said to have been built by the Giant Cormoran, or rather by his wife, Cormelian, whom he bullied into carrying huge granite blocks from the Penwith moors in her leather apron. One day as he dozed lazily on the hillside she decided to carry a great piece of greenstone which she found lying nearby, rather than trudge all the way back to the moor; but, waking up to what she was doing, Cormoran

administered her a kick which sent her sprawling
and broke her apron strings. The greenstone fell
some way short of the Mount, and hundreds of
years later, when the sea rushed in and engulfed
the area, the rock was left showing above the tide.

Another fearsome giant was Bolster, who in one
stride could step from St Agnes Beacon to Carn
Brea – about six miles. He fell in love with the
beautiful Saint Agnes herself, and to escape his
attentions she demanded that he should fill a great
hole in the cliff with his blood. The besotted giant
cut one of his veins and bled to death, not realising
that the bottom of the hole was connected to the
sea by a small tunnel.

But the most famous figure in Cornish folklore is
the ghost of Jan Tregeagle, who for his sins is
hunted across Bodmin Moor by the Devil and his
dogs. Tregeagle, the unjust Steward of the Lord of
Lanhydrock, is reputed to have robbed his master
of lands and extorted unfair rents from his tenants.

WILL BROIL YOU FOR MY BREAKFAST.

*Left: the giant Bolster strides from St Agnes Beacon to
Carn Brea. This page, top: Jack 'the giant-killer' lures
Cormoran to his death in a pit on St Michael's Mount.
Right: Jan Tregeagle, sentenced to a series of grim tasks,
drops a sack of sand and creates Loe Bar. Finally, he
was condemned to bale out Dozmary Pool (above) with
a limpet shell with a hole in it*

After his death he was first sentenced to carry sacks
of sand from Porthleven to Marazion, and dropped
one across the mouth of the Cober River, creating
the Loe Bar. He was then set to spin sheaves of
sand at the mouth of the River Camel, but
annoyed the people of Padstow and St Minver,
and was shut into an oven at Trevorder; his
bellowings disturbed the peace of St Breock and
Wadebridge, so he was finally, with the aid of

monks and priests, established at Dozmary Pool near Jamaica Inn, and condemned to bale it out with a limpet shell with a hole in it. But on the wildest nights he is hunted across the Moor by a pack of satanic hounds.

The true story of Tregeagle emerges from no less than five successive generations of John Tregeagles who were active in the 16th to 18th centuries in mid-Cornwall. The first was indeed steward to Lord Robartes at Lanhydrock, and established a reputation as a severe magistrate. The second and third, his son and grandson, were Receivers-General to the Duchy of Cornwall and involved in a financial scandal. The combination of ill repute and apparent immortality has created the legend, embellished by the many 'droll-tellers' who travelled about, amusing cottagers with such stories at their firesides in winter.

Tales of the piskies are found in most parts of Cornwall. At St Allen near Truro a nine-year-old boy vanished for three weeks, and was then found asleep but unharmed in a bed of ferns; he told how he was taken away by the Little People into a palace of gold and silver and fed on fairy food. There are many accounts of people being 'pisky-led' – wandering around a field unable to find the gate, or led a dance over moorlands and becoming disorientated. In North Cornwall piskies were reputed to ride horses at night until they became exhausted; in West Cornwall cows would be milked dry at night.

Another story concerns an old furze-cutter who came across a tiny creature dressed in green cloth with diamond buckled shoes, asleep in the gorse. He took the little fellow home and kept him to entertain the family – he was a fine dancer – but the children let him out one day and he was claimed back by his own people. To have a pisky in the house always brought good fortune.

The spirits of the mines, known as Buccas or Knockers, were well-treated by the miners who always left underground a portion of their pasties or 'fuggans' (dough-cake) for them. Their

Tales of the Little People abound in Cornwall

There are many Cornish tales involving mermaids

knockings served as warnings of impending danger or rock-falls. The Buccas were said to be the spirits of Jews who had worked at smelting tin in Cornwall, and who were consigned after their deaths neither to Heaven nor Hell but a limbo in the tin mines.

Mermaids feature prominently in Cornish folklore. The Mermaid of Padstow, having lured a local fisherman into her embraces, was shot by him when he attempted to escape from her spell. In her dying moments she cursed the port – a terrible storm then raged, destroying many vessels, and threw up the great bank of sand known as the Doom Bar, on which hundreds of ships foundered during the centuries. The Mermaid of Zennor actually went to church and fell in love with the leading tenor in the choir, Mathy Trewhella; she successfully lured him down to the ocean bed, where he married her and had mer-children. At Cury near the Lizard an old man called Lutey found a stranded mermaid and helped her back into the sea, where she swam away to rejoin her merman husband and children, but not before she had granted Lutey three wishes. He would be immune to the spells of witchcraft, able to gain knowledge from the spirits, and his family would possess these powers for all posterity. But the sea-sprite told him she would come back to take him down to the sea-kingdoms with her, and nine years after the day she did re-appear, and the bewitched old man vanished with her into the waves.

Legends of lost cities around the coast of Cornwall undoubtedly represent folk-memories of inundations during the past. Between Land's End and the Scillies is claimed to lie the fabled land of Lyonesse, drowned in AD1099, and the bells of churches are said to have been heard ringing beneath the waters. Between Crantock and Perranporth once existed the great city of Langarroc. It was said to have been covered up by sand in a great storm about a thousand years ago, when most of its inhabitants perished, a punishment for their evil doings.

Encroaching sand has always been a great problem along the North Cornish coast, and St Piran's Oratory near Perranporth, a tiny chapel originally built by the saint himself about AD490, was for centuries covered up. Excavated in 1835, it was claimed to be the oldest extant building of Christian worship on mainland Britain – the second oldest after Iona Abbey. A long battle was fought to drain it and clear it of sand, but today, in order to protect it, the oratory has sadly been reburied and is now marked only by a rough stone saying simply 'St Piran'.

The saint was one of the hundreds of holy men and women who came to Cornwall from Ireland,

Above: St Piran's Oratory about 1900. Now it has been reburied. Left: St Neot was a pigmy. His life is told in the stained glass windows of St Neot's Church

Patron Saint of Cornish Miners, in celebration and commemoration of his discovery of how to smelt tin: one cold night he built up a bigger fire than usual in his cave on the foreshore at Perranzabuloe – 'St Piran in the Sands' – and a large black hearthstone cracked asunder in the heat, giving forth shining white tin metal. The Cornish Flag, a white cross on a black background, is thus named after him.

Among other notable saints was the virgin St Keyne, who blessed a well in the parish named after her in south-east Cornwall, and dedicated it to marriage. A poem by Robert Southey celebrates this: after the wedding husband and wife would rush to drink the well water, for 'he who first the water drinks, the mastery shall gain'. St Neot, whose church stands in a beautiful secluded valley near Liskeard, was a pigmy about 3 ft high, whose life is remembered in the glorious mediaeval stained glass windows surviving in the church.

But the greatest Cornish saint was undoubtedly St Petroc, patron of Padstow and Bodmin, who established powerful monasteries at both places. He is said to have tamed the last great dragon ravaging the Cornish countryside, and binding his stole around its neck, mercifully led it to the sea near Padstow where it swam away. He also cast a spell over the warlike Prince Constantine who was hunting a little fawn and, converting him to Christianity, commanded him to spend the rest of his days in poverty and prayer at a cell near the bay named after him. The holy well of St Constantine and the remains of his mediaeval church can be seen among the dunes on Trevose Golf Course.

The relics of St Petroc were so venerated that in the 12th century a monk stole them and took them to St Méen across the Channel; Henry II of England, the Overlord of Brittany, commanded their return and gave a richly carved ivory casket in which to keep them.

Perhaps the most fascinating of all legends is that

Wales or Brittany, sister Celtic countries, between AD490 and AD650 – the 'Age of the Saints'. The saying goes that 'there are more saints in Cornwall than in Heaven', for every other village seems to be named after a saint, usually an obscure one about whom little is known. During the Dark and early Middle Ages the term 'saint' was used for a respected holy man or woman who had founded a cell and ministered to the local populace. Some of these were, however, great saints who have been recognised by the Catholic and Anglican churches, among them St Piran, who was widely venerated in mediaeval times.

He came, it is believed, from Ireland, and according to legend lived a roistering life, fond of his tipple, and died at the ripe old age of 206 by falling into a well when drunk one night. He is the

of King Arthur, who was mortally wounded fighting his last battle against his treacherous nephew, Mordred. Many places in Britain claim Arthur, the great British hero who defeated the Saxons in 12 successive battles, but the tradition that he was actually a Cornishman has been strong in Cornwall since mediaeval times.

So tenacious were the Cornish in their belief that he would come again one day to rescue them from bondage that in AD1177 there was a riot in Bodmin church between visiting French monks and the local men; a Frenchman had scoffed at such an article of faith. The spirit of Arthur was believed to fly over the cliffs of Cornwall in the form of the Cornish chough – a bird now extinct in the county except for two or three pairs in captivity, at Padstow Bird Gardens and Newquay Zoo.

Tintagel Castle is the usual scene of Arthur's birth in romance and legend. Geoffrey of Monmouth, 12th-century author of the *History of the Kings of Britain*, was the first to record this belief. Evidence of a Celtic royal household has been found, but the remains of the castle there today, starkly situated on its island above towering cliffs, are Norman in origin. Another tradition associated Arthur with Castle-an-Dinas near St Columb, the

The myth of King Arthur has inspired writers and artists alike. The painting below portrays his death, the legendary site for which is at Camelford, near Slaughterbridge, where there is an engraved stone, the so-called 'Arthur's Tomb'

largest Celtic hill fort in Cornwall, which was also known as the seat of Cornish kings after Arthur's time. (Castle-an-Dinas has now been acquired from the Duchy of Cornwall by the Cornwall Heritage Trust, for opening to the public.)

Arthur's last battle was fought, according to Cornish legend, at Slaughterbridge near Camelford, where the river ran crimson with the blood of slain warriors. Sir Bedivere was sent to Dozmary Pool, six miles away on the moors, to return the sword Excalibur to the waters. And in the imagination of Alfred Lord Tennyson, the dying Arthur was carried down to the narrow loch-like harbour of Boscastle to be taken away in the funeral barge to Avalon.

Another legend, one of the greatest of love stories, has been given by Cornwall to the world: that of Tristan and Iseult, who shared the love potion mean for Iseult and her future husband, King Mark, and so were doomed to an illicit passion. Near Fowey is the stone inscribed with the earliest known form of the name Tristan, and not far from Helston in Meneage is a ford which was recorded as *Hryt Eselt* in the 10th century – the earliest known form of Iseult. King Mark, who sent Tristan to Ireland to bring Iseult back to be his queen, is traditionally associated with Castle Dore near Galant. And the earliest form of the romance, by the Norman-French poet, Béroul, sets the story firmly in south and mid-Cornwall, mentioning places such as Chapel Rock near Mevagissey (Tristan's Leap) and the Forest of Morrois (Moresk, near Truro), where the lovers fled to hide from Mark and his barons.

Cornish Wildlife

Algae and barnacles beside a rock pool on an exposed stretch of seashore.
Inset: a shore crab brandishes its pincers

Cornwall is almost an island, cut off from the rest of the country by the River Tamar. Its Atlantic situation as the most south-westerly part of England results in a relatively warm, wet climate with strong winds sweeping across the land. The county's natural history is influenced by these factors as well as by geology, and a number of exciting contrasts result, as can be seen easily enough when one travels about.

An obvious contrast is between the north coast and the south. The one is stark and wild with high, bare cliffs and few harbours. The other is gentler and more broken with numerous estuaries where wooded valleys run down to the sea – most of Cornwall's rivers flow southwards from the moors. Where breaks in the line of cliffs permit, as near Perranporth, there are more extensive sand-dunes on the north coast, with their own particular flora including burnet rose, sea rocket and sea holly. Salt-marshes, where sea spurrey and sea asters grow, are more frequent in the south. Beaches everywhere are regularly covered and uncovered by the tides to reveal the different

phases in the life of the seashore, with zoned banks of different seaweeds and the shelled creatures that live among them.

There are contrasts along the north coast itself where bare rock faces alternate with strips and cushions of brightly coloured flowers; and the stunted oak forest of the Dizzard, which stretches down landslip slopes almost to sea-level, has beside it some of the most uncompromising cliffs in Cornwall. Inland there are cultivated farmlands adjacent to industrial dereliction, the relics of china-clay workings and tin-mining in past centuries.

Above right: a fulmar in flight, its effortless gliding a familiar sight along the clifftops.
Above left: the burnet rose, a low-growing shrub 6–18in. high, forms large patches, especially in sand dunes

There are deep-cut ferny lanes with great splashes of colour provided by foxgloves, red campion and other colourful flowers; and mature old valley hardwoods contrasting with moorlands which look more barren than they really are, as the boggy ground supports numerous flowers. Cornwall's 'hedges' (stone walls) are almost bare on the windward side except for lichens, but full of colour on the other with stonecrops, rock spurrey and gorse. On walls, or wherever there are crevices, it is worth looking for ferns as the spleenworts in Cornwall include the rare bright green lanceolate spleenwort. Different again is the open water of Dozmary Pool and several reservoirs where great flocks of wildfowl pass the winter.

There are also many other wetland areas, among them Breney Common and Red Moor, near Bodmin, both owned and managed as reserves by the county Nature Conservation Trust. They are areas of heathland, ponds and willow carr where the trees grow in damp ground with reeds, rushes, mosses and the splendid royal fern; birds, including tits and such migrant warblers as the chiff-chaff, nest among the branches. A rich and varied animal life occupies the ponds, which have frogs, toads, palmate newts and countless invertebrates. Among the latter are diving and whirligig beetles, water boatmen, which swim on their boat-shaped backs, and Britain's only water-spider, which spins an air-filled 'diving bell' where it lives and breathes below the surface.

Soils are generally more acid than alkaline and relate to the underlying granite or to sedimentary rock formations; the latter are mainly Devonian shales and sandstones, known as 'killas', or the carboniferous culm measures of north-east Cornwall. These are the remains of the heavily faulted Armorican mountain chain which stretched down south-west Britain some two hundred million years ago. Molten rock from the earth's interior welled up into the mountains, cooled and solidified until, exposed by erosion, it became the granite spine of the county (and of Devon): Bodmin and other moorland areas, West Penwith and the Isles of Scilly. There are a few exposures of volcanic rock, notably the pillow lava of Pentire Head, and the ancient pre-Cambrian rocks of the Lizard peninsula. There is very little limestone.

The rocks of the Lizard are mainly serpentine, gabbro and schists. They support a unique flora which makes this area one of Britain's classic botanical sites. Plants of special interest include Cornish heath (*Erica vagans*), pygmy rush, orchids and rare members of both clover and buttercup families; prostrate wild asparagus grows on a rocky islet off Kynance Cove. The level of the sea in relation to the land has varied greatly through the

Britain's only water-spider is found in ponds in some of Cornwall's wetland areas

during migration periods. Shelduck, among the most colourful of British wildfowl, also favour such places and sometimes nest in rabbit burrows along the verges.

Part of the charm of Cornwall's long coastline is that it offers many different kinds of beach – some rocky, others sandy or strewn with boulders, stones or pebbles – the degree of exposure to the waves and the weather varying greatly between beaches. Such factors determine the kind and abundance of seaweeds and of the marine animals likely to be found in rock-pools or attached to

Ornithologists are urgently trying to prevent the puffin (above left) becoming extinct in Cornwall
Above right: the dog whelk with its mass of egg capsules

ages, and this has produced a series of ancient marine platforms which is why a large part of Cornwall appears so flat.

In the spring and early summer the wild flowers of the coast are astonishing in their abundance and variety and can be seen at their best from the Coast Path. Cliff tops and exposed edges are outlined with thrift. Buttercups, violets, spring squill, sheep's sorrel and self-heal colour the maritime grassland. Gorse and hawthorn scrub are in full flower – thyme, western gorse and another range of plants appear later in the year to continue the panorama. Heathers are plentiful in some areas. Between bands of scurvy grass the cliff faces are bright yellow with flowers of bird's-foot trefoil and kidney vetch, variety being added by wild carrot, rock samphire and sea campion. At lower levels, where the influence of the sea is direct, there are sea lavender, orange lichens and green algae. In places bluebells and primroses, away from their normal woodland habitat, grow surprisingly close to the sea.

The birds are almost equally attractive. Gulls breed all along the coast, the main concentration of the beautifully sleek kittiwake being on St Agnes Head. Fulmars share some of their breeding cliffs, and there are a few pairs of that master falcon, the peregrine. Kestrels, buzzards and ravens are seen less often than they used to be but are still present. Auks do not breed north of Beeny, near Boscastle, but the commonest of them, razorbills and guillemots, are reasonably plentiful south and west of that point. There are very few puffins left thanks largely to the curse of oil pollution. Shags and oystercatchers occupy rocky beaches and sandy shores respectively. Choughs are now extinct in Cornwall but jackdaws are ubiquitous. Small songbirds are plentiful in the clifftop furze, while waders, such as sandpipers and godwits, are best seen on estuaries and salt-marshes in winter or

rocks. Mussels, barnacles, limpets, whelks, crabs and anemones are widely distributed. Ocean currents sometimes bring transatlantic species to Cornwall's shores, among them jellyfish-like animals and octopods. Whales and dolphins sometimes visit the coast or strand themselves on the beaches.

Of greater local interest, however, are the grey (or Atlantic) seals which breed on a few inaccessible stony beaches and in sea caves. They are a delight to watch as they hunt for fish or haul out on to their favourite rocky platforms, particularly when assembled during the autumn breeding season. The bulls arrive first to establish their territories and collect as many females as they can attract. Many of the females are already pregnant from last year's mating and drop their pups soon after joining the bull. They stay with their babies for about three weeks when these should be weaned and robust enough to fend for themselves in the sea. By this time the mother seal is ready to mate again, mating usually taking place in the water. The seals then disperse. At birth, baby seals have long silky white hair which they moult when fully weaned. Particularly when the weather is rough, these quite charming white babies can become separated from their mothers, and you sometimes find them apparently abandoned on various Cornish beaches. It is best to leave them where they are as the mother usually follows her baby out to sea and is likely to be somewhere nearby waiting for darkness and the high tide.

The greatest concentration of seals is on the Isles of Scilly where also there are very large numbers of breeding sea birds, mainly on outlying islands and sea-stacks – for instance, both storm petrels and Manx shearwaters breed on Annet Island. Several common land birds are absent but rare visitors from North America, blown off course across the Atlantic, appear so often that searching for and watching rare birds on the islands has become a well-established branch of the tourist industry. Another interest – this time for botanically-minded visitors – lies in deciding which of the many plants they find are genuine natives and not unusual garden escapes; there are several local varieties of wild plants on the islands. There is also a Scilly shrew, not found on the mainland, which is hunted by rats on stony beaches and, for the lepidopterist, there is a local sub-species of the familiar meadow brown butterfly.

There is more to Cornwall than the coast, though no place is more than 15 miles from the sea, and the hinterland is dominated by the granite moors which reach their highest point on Brown Willy (1371ft). There are rocky tors and clitter slopes but most of the open land has been so improved for grazing that little heather is left and only scattered bilberry bushes remain. Many bogs have been drained; those that survive support an interesting flora with sphagnum moss, cotton grass, bog asphodel, orchids, insect-devouring sundews and much else besides. Pools and streams, often bordered by ferns, provide yet another colourful scene; yellow flags contrast with purple marsh orchids and blue forget-me-nots, while several species of dragonfly hawk for insects. Too many of the woods which used to occupy the margins of the moors have been cleared away.

There are numerous heathlands, both dry and wet, away from the main moorland areas, and they are very characteristic inland Cornish habitats. Dry heath has often developed on land laid waste by former tin-mining and streaming activities and is typified by the common ling heather, with minute leaves and pink flowers, as well as the purple-flowered bell heather. The now rare Dorset heath grows in a few such places. Wet heathland, which occurs in relatively small patches throughout the county, is dominated by purple moor grass; if any heather occurs it is most likely to be the cross-leaved heath. Heath spotted orchids are fairly common.

The yellow flag iris thrives beside Cornwall's pools and streams

Numerous insects thrive in such surroundings with marsh fritillary butterflies, bush crickets, grasshoppers, blue agrion damselflies and four-spotted hawker dragonflies among the most attractive. Spiders are numerous.

The bird life of the higher moors tends to be dominated in the winter by large flocks of lapwings, golden plovers and curlews, solitary pairs of which breed in many moorland valleys. Meadow pipits, which are often parasitized by cuckoos, are the commonest small bird of the open moor; linnets, stonechats and skylarks are also widespread. Foxes are widespread; badgers make their setts among the boulders. Several butterflies occur, among them the uncommon green hairstreak, whose caterpillars feed on gorse and bilberries, and the dark green fritillary which is associated with violets.

Most of the ancient woods in Cornwall are dominated by sessile oak (which has stalkless acorns) with ash, holly and other trees. A few of those that survive were mentioned in the Domesday Survey; other woods unfortunately have been cleared away to make room for conifer plantations, farming, mining and even building development. Among those that remain, Drayne's near Liskeard, Pelyn near Lostwithiel, Lanhydrock near Bodmin and the valley woods of the south coast are the most important; and conservation of the remaining deciduous woods is now a vital task. They support a rich and varied ground flora with mosses, ferns, fungi and, among lichens, the large plate-shaped tree lungwort which shows the relative absence of pollution in the atmosphere. Among flowering plants are wood anemones, bluebells and snowdrops.

The bird and animal life of Cornish woods is generally similar to that found in damp valley woods elsewhere, with badgers, foxes, stoats and weasels. The insect life includes many woodland butterflies. Otters, which are becoming increasingly rare in Britain, still inhabit a few Cornish rivers, mainly where the banks are well wooded, and they may eventually be re-introduced elsewhere now

The green hairstreak butterfly at rest, showing its green underwings streaked with a fine white line. It appears in May and June, mainly in woodland

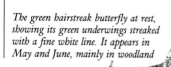

Above: Cornwall is one of the few areas of Britain where the otter is still found.
Left: the southern marsh orchid

that a branch of The Otter Trust has been established near Launceston. It is to be hoped that competition from the alien mink, now widely distributed, will not prove too strong. Red deer occur in certain woodland areas in east Cornwall.

The delightful badger is normally looked upon as a beneficial species, but was believed to be responsible for the spread of bovine tuberculosis in West Penwith and in the east of the county during the 1970s. Badger setts were gassed and hundreds of animals killed in an attempt to wipe out the disease. This is a highly complex issue about which much could be written, but naturalists did not believe that badgers were the guilty parties and at the time of writing the killing of badgers has almost ceased – without any apparent increase in the

The grey seal, Britain's largest wild mammal, comes ashore only to breed and to bask

spread of tuberculosis among cattle. The argument continues. Badgers in Cornwall are found not only in woods and on the moors; they are quite plentiful in coastal scrub.

What is being done to preserve all this wildlife?

Firstly, the Nature Conservancy Council, the Government's official watchdog, has listed more than 60 Sites of Special Scientific Interest and has established the Lizard National Nature Reserve, covering 1,000 acres of valuable heathland. The National Trust owns over a hundred miles of coast, including some of the best areas, like Pentire Head and Dodman Point, and some fine old deciduous woods inland. The Cornwall Bird Watching and Preservation Society owns two sanctuaries and leases the rights over parts of certain reservoirs where wildfowl and waders feed. The Cornwall Trust for Nature Conservation, the one body concerned with all forms of nature conservation throughout the county, owns or leases or manages 28 nature reserves covering some 3,000 acres, most of Cornwall's major habitats being represented. Many other areas are carefully monitored. Cornwall, moreover, is fortunate in the co-operative attitude of County and District Councils, but pressures remain formidable.

Gardens

Those travellers with a keen eye for the landscape who make the journey from London or the north towards the south-west will appreciate the rich pastures of Somerset and the lush beauty of lowland Devon. Continuing westwards across the Tamar and on down the long peninsula of Cornwall might well raise expectations of a land even more exotic in garden and hedgerow.

At first sight the very reverse would appear to be true. For Devon's rolling hills, its rich red earth, its high hedges and narrow lanes soon give way to a bleak granite upland, effectively separating north coast from south. So it is that many of the Duchy's summer visitors return home with memories of a coastline that is incomparable (especially if the weather has been clement), but of an interior that is nothing but an uninviting windswept moorland.

If this is so they have not travelled wisely, for this superficially forbidding land is one of only two areas in the islands of Great Britain (the other is a narrow maritime belt of western Scotland) that are genuinely able to grow plants from warm temperate climates out of doors.

To the south of the central spine of granite and moors there is some shelter from the worst of the great westerly gales. The land descends gradually in rolling 'downs' to a coastline that is generally far less rugged than the north. The short-lived streams that cut their way through the downs, such as the Lynher, the Fowey and the Fal soon become deep-water estuaries enclosing a system of inlets and drowned valleys penetrating well inland. The Fal is the finest example of these drowned valleys, where a complex of beautiful, wooded creeks meets to form the great estuary of the Carrick Roads. It is along this coast from the Tamar to the Helford and again in the south-facing part of Mount's Bay that the effect of the Gulf Stream is most pronounced. The climate is relatively mild with a high humidity; frost and snow are rare and fleeting. Almost as important for the gardener, the

Main picture: the dovecote and pool at Cotehele
Inset: as the rhododendrons at Tregothnan near the end of the flowering period, the paths are strewn with petals

moderating effect of the sea temperature ensures a relatively cool summer. The final part of the pattern is set by the way in which the various forms of mainly Devonian rock weather into a strongly acid soil so essential for the cultivation of many exotic plants.

It was mainly in these secluded southern valleys that the great gardens of Cornwall were developed. The perceptive will notice the bewildering pockets of 'micro-climate' often magnified by cunningly sited planting of shelter belts. Some who garden in the small area between Truro and the Helford describe it as 'the banana belt' (a title that can most kindly be described as unproven).

Up-country enthusiasts intent on discovering as much of the best of the botanical treasures as he or she or both may have time for will ask: 'When is the best time to come?' A good question indeed! March for the camellias, April for the magnolias, May for the rhododendrons – unless the spring is very mild or very cold. A good compromise is the last week in April and the first in May.

Start your tour from the Cornish side of the Tamar Bridge. Lining the western side of that broad river, on strategic sites overlooking the Sound or commanding some of the many miles of creek are a number of great houses with gardens which, if not entirely in the Cornish tradition, should not be missed: Cotehele, Ince Castle, Port Eliot, Antony House and Mount Edgcumbe. There is not space here to do justice to all these and if only a few miles apart as the crow flies they involve long detours by road. *Mount Edgcumbe* with its wonderful views across the Sound to Plymouth is now a country park covering nearly

900 acres and open every day of the year. Unique in Cornwall are the magnificent formal gardens containing many rare plants in landscaped settings. Here, too, the National Camellia Collection is being established. It is only too easy to believe that Mount Edgcumbe was coveted by Medina Sidonia, Commander of the Spanish Armada who swore he would live there if the English were defeated. On the River Lynher is *Ince Castle*, perhaps the only major brick building in Cornwall. The gardens of about five acres are of relatively recent creation but already have great charm and are well worth a visit.

Follow the main road to Liskeard and then turn off towards the coast and *Caerhays Castle*. Caerhays is the mecca of all those who enjoy the three Cornish staples: the camellia, magnolia and rhododendron. Here, on a great sloping hillside 100 acres in extent and leading down to the very edge of the sea is one of the world's great collections of these, and much else besides. Three generations of the Williams family, beginning with the renowned John Charles Williams (chief sponsor of such supreme plant collectors as Forrest and Wilson), created this garden. Not only were hundreds of seedlings planted but 'J.C.' alone made some 250 rhododendron crosses of which barely 3 per cent have been named. Nor is this prodigious raiser remembered for his rhododendrons alone, for his interest in this field began with daffodils and included camellias in great number. There are few gardeners who do not know of the *Williamsii camellias* or the *Williamsianum rhododendron*. Caerhays is the plantsman's paradise.

Back now along the winding lanes between the Cornish hedges covered in spring with sheets of wild flowers to the A390 and *Trewithen*. It is sometimes referred to as Cornwall's most beautiful garden – an impossible assessment to make, but there is no doubt that here the visitor will discover a veritable treasure trove of rare and tender plants

A spring carpet of many colours in one of Cornwall's most delightful gardens, Trewithen

growing to perfection and superbly maintained. Unusually for Cornwall, the garden is mainly level, its most striking feature being the lawn which stretches away from the fine, early Georgian house for 200 yards, its gently curving edges framed by great banks of rhododendron overhung by magnolia after magnolia, the perfection of which is a reflection of the garden's creator, George Johnstone, for whom they were his special interest. Do not miss the *Rhododendron macabeanum* reputably and deservedly Britain's finest form of this deep-yellow flowered species.

Continuing on your way south and west, much of the woodland to the left of the road belongs to the *Tregothnan* estate, the gardens of which are open to the public only twice a year in spring. They are ever-increasingly worth a visit, the great lawns backed by proportionately sized scarlet rhododendrons up to a century old. This great garden/park of some 80 acres enjoys a continuing planting process which ensures something new and something more every year.

A few miles farther on, past the triple-spired cathedral at Truro, and a brief detour brings us to *Trelissick*, one of the leading gardens of the National Trust in Cornwall. High above the deep, salt-water inlet formed by the Fal there are splendid panoramic views across the Carrick Roads to Pendennis Castle. Trelissick is also a summer garden renowned for its collection of species hydrangea.

To the south of Falmouth we enter the 'Fox country'. To that town in 1759 came George Croker Fox, a Quaker merchant and banker who prospered mightily so that by the turn of the century the family was spreading out around the town and very shortly owned eight fine estates all within a radius of some five miles. Three of these estates developed outstanding gardens with some characteristics in common – one being that they stood at the head of deep valleys running down to the sea or the Helford River. The parent garden was *Penjerrick*, the story of which is as romantic as any in our gardening history. Here, the soil is

Top: the maze at Glendurgan, planted by Alfred Fox in 1883 with laurel, an unusual choice
Above: early morning mist in the valley at Trebah

deep, never drying out and never flooding. The eye is led down a lawn flanked by purple beeches and contrasting conifers framing the sea a mile away. The rate of growth is prolific and the dense planting provides a near-tropical effect. It was at Penjerrick that Samuel Smith, head gardener for half a century, produced the glorious Penjerrick hybrid rhododendrons. It is said that though distributed among many gardens in England and Scotland nowhere do the Penjerrick hybrids flower as they do on their native soil. Still to be seen (and in increasing need of careful maintenance), are the original shrubs which were the product of these crossings.

Glendurgan shared in many of the botanical treasures from Penjerrick whilst developing its own atmosphere. Of particular interest are enormous specimens of liriodendron (the tulip tree) and a huge range of camellias and magnolias. At the foot of the garden is the tiny village of Durgan, a jewel of a place and not to be missed at any time of year. A few hundred yards from Glendurgan is the third of the great Fox gardens, *Trebah*. A major planting exercise is in hand to restore the depleted shelter belt so vital to all Cornish gardens. Everywhere the views are breathtaking. A small stream provides a water garden as far as the neck of the ravine which is packed with rhododendrons and camellias, many of enormous size and perhaps a hundred years old. From the terrace in spring one looks down on a vast carpet of many colours, for once seeing these flowering trees from above. Graded paths wind down each side of the ravine, which provides almost entirely frost-free shelter for tender Asiatic

and Australasian plants with the tree fern *Dicksonia antarctica* growing in abundance.

Just outside the historic town of Helston, in a secluded valley is *Trevarno*. Here is another truly superb woodland garden not to be missed. Trevarno opens on several days in April and May and comprises several acres of gently terraced gardens crammed with rare plants and especially interesting for the remarkably comprehensive and excitingly planted conifers, many very rare in cultivation. A large ornamental lake at the foot of the garden makes a perfect foil for rich and continuing planting.

Along the coast of Mount's Bay, *St Michael's Mount* can be mentioned in the gardening context for, very occasionally, Lord and Lady St Levan open their private gardens to the public. If your visit coincides with such an opening do not miss it! Situated on a series of narrow terraces suspended between the rocky shore below and the fairy-tale silver granite walls of the castle 250ft above, a new, rapidly expanding and improving garden is taking shape where many tender plants too numerous to mention successfully defy the salt spray of winter storms.

Through Penzance and just off the road to Land's End is *Trengwainton*. It was founded on the wealth from the slave trade; Wilberforce's Act (which ended the slave trade) ruined the original owner and Trengwainton passed to the Bolitho family. It is now run by the National Trust. Perhaps the most frost-free garden on the mainland of Britain, Trengwainton can lay claim to its most comprehensive collection of rare, sub-tropical plants able to be grown outdoors. Near the entrance to the drive is a complex of five walled gardens providing almost total shelter for these rarities. The long drive itself is flanked by a tumbling stream lavishly planted with massed primulas, meconopsis and many other water and bog species, backed by massed rhododendrons both species and hybrids. Around the house are some of the finest magnolias in Cornwall. A mainly 20th-century garden, Trengwainton owed much to the gift of plants and good advice from the other owners of estate gardens in the county.

A great many splendid gardens, large and small, must perforce be left undescribed. *Bosahan*, for instance, on the opposite side of the Helford to Trebah and offering equally superb views and dramatic sub-tropical effect. *Chyverton*, near the north coast and sheltered by fine woodlands, begun in the 1790s and planted up continually ever since, has a collection of typical Cornish plants to complement that of Caerhays itself. It is open by appointment. Much farther to the north in seemingly inhospitable country is the smaller garden of *Tremeer*, where six acres of vivid colour and pervading scent are set between the Atlantic and Bodmin Moor.

There are many, many others, especially the newer, smaller gardens made between or after the wars.

Information on National Trust gardens is given in the Directory, page 82. Except where specified, most of the other gardens described are open only during the peak flowering period, in April, May and June.

The Cornwall Garden Society produces a 'Gardens Open Calendar' annually in February (price 50p) which gives most of the information visitors will need. It can be obtained from The Secretary, 'Chysbryn', Bareppa, Mawnan Smith, Falmouth, Cornwall. Please send 50p and a large, stamped, addressed envelope.

Long Distance Footpaths

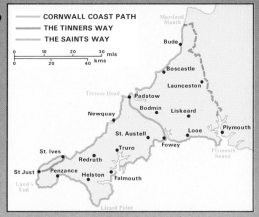

Cornwall's coastline, its wild flowers, its scenery make exploration on foot a must. Around the coast runs the 268-mile Cornwall Coast Path; inland are the 30-mile Saints' Way and the less well-defined 13-mile Tinners' Way, based on routes used by people for over a thousand years. All lend themselves to short explorations along sections of their lengths.

Cornwall Coast Path

The Cornwall Coast Path is 268 miles long and runs from Marsland Mouth on the north coast round Land's End and on to the shores of Plymouth Sound. It is the central part of the 520-mile South West Way, the longest continuous footpath in England.

Like the whole of the South West Way, the Cornwall Coast Path is usually walked from north to south, a psychologically 'downhill' journey that leads the walker from the great 600ft cliffs at Marsland to the granite knuckle of the Land's End Peninsula then back to the east, along the gentler south coast.

Physically, the CCP is one of the most challenging expeditions in the country. It lacks the great heights of the mountain footpaths, but in total demands such a series of ups and downs that it could match Everest foot by uphill foot!

Main picture: view from the Cornwall Coast Path over Kynance Cove.
Inset, this page: on the clifftop path near Zennor.
Inset, opposite page: the sun sets beyond Cape Cornwall

How the path began

Much of the Cornwall Coast Path is based on the tracks that marked out the regular 'beats' walked by coastguards. In 1947, a new National Parks Committee suggested that a continuous pathway round the British coast was a possibility. Cornwall offered the ideal conditions for a continuous county path but it was not until May 1973 that the Cornwall Coast Path was officially opened.

Since then there have been steady improvements so that today a continuous route is open to the experienced walker as a challenging journey of unsurpassed beauty and variety.

On the way

The Cornwall Coast Path can be divided into three convenient sections for both planning and description's sake.

The first is from Marsland Mouth on the Devon border to St Ives in Penwith, a distance of 112 miles. The second is from St Ives, via Land's End and Penzance, to the Lizard, a distance of 64 miles. The third is from the Lizard to Plymouth, a 92-mile final section.

All three sections are quite different in character, their underlying geology dictating the type of landscape and coastal formations, and in many cases the local natural environment.

Marsland Mouth to St Ives (112 miles)

Imperceptibly the main South West Way leaves Devon at Marsland Mouth and enters Cornwall to follow the western edge of that enchanting northern extension of the county, bounded by the infant River Tamar on the east and the Atlantic on the west.

This is not yet Celtic Cornwall, more a unique little island in its own right, remote and particularly lovely. The great cliffs of the culm-measures buttress the coast at Marsland and Sharpnose, where black fins of rock thrust seawards from the main cliff. The path leads across occasional valley bottoms by Morwenstow and Coombe and so on to Bude, the first of the great breaks in the coast, where vast sands stretch into the distance at low tide and the huge Atlantic breakers thunder on to the shoreline.

Beyond Bude the route is marred in places by land-slip and diversion. It is easily navigable, however, and graced with superb views as it leads the walker to the more isolated sections at Buckator and Beeny Cliff before Boscastle is reached in the lovely Valency Valley. The coast is less dramatic than the previous section but equally fascinating.

Beyond Boscastle with its strange chasm-like

harbour lies the 'romantic' Tintagel, awash with Arthurian myth and unashamed commercialism. Crowds and cream teas are soon left behind for the magnificent stretch of coast that leads on to the Camel Estuary, another major inlet on the Cornish coast.

For the walker, the estuary is approached via the splendid Rumps Point and Pentire Point where there are breathtaking views across the infamous Doom Bar to Stepper Point and Trevose Head. In summer a passenger ferry will transport the walker from Rock to the busy and charming port of Padstow, whence the Saints' Way leads across Cornwall to Fowey on the south coast.

From Padstow, the CCP leads to Trevose Head and on towards Newquay, past superb beaches where sprawling holiday developments are balanced by the wild magnificence of such places as Park Head and Bedruthan Steps.

At Newquay, the walker can pause for a while to savour once more the necessary contrast between the various tourist needs. Beyond here the coast is again particularly lovely as the path follows the edge of great beaches and traverses green-backed headlands towards the strange industrial landscape of the St Agnes mining coast, then goes onwards to Godrevy Point, the northern outlier of St Ives Bay and the gateway to the Land's End Peninsula.

St Ives to the Lizard (64 miles)

The lovely town of St Ives is forever linked to the Cornish fishing industry, a trade that has shaped the character of the modern town as both tourist resort and artists' haven. Beyond here the walker enters the Land's End Peninsula along the wildest and most remote part of the coast path as it winds its way towards the west, by greenstone and granite cliff above seas of aquamarine and beautiful beaches of white shell-sand.

Here the ancient moorland of Penwith rises steeply from the coastal shelf by Zennor and Morvah, where farming is still carried on within the same fields that Iron Age settlers used. It is an area particularly rich in ancient memorials, where stone circles, burial 'quoits' and Iron Age villages have survived, partly because of their granite resilience, although much more has been lost by plunder and carelessness. The National Trust plays a vital part in conserving the important landscape features which remain and in 1986 launched a £200,000 appeal.

This remarkable stretch of the coast path includes the desolate industrial landscape round Pendeen and St Just, an area that was once a mining heartland but is now sadly redundant since the closure (1986) of Geevor Mine, Cornwall's last coastal working. There the landscape has a desolation that is not without its own rather strange attractiveness.

Several miles beyond here lies Land's End, the attractions of which may be diminished for the walker after the miles of beautiful coastline already covered.

Here the walker turns away from the Atlantic coast along the finest granite cliffs of all, by Gwennap Head and Porthcurno, and on to the busy town of Penzance and Mount's Bay, dominated by the offshore island of St Michael's Mount with its splendid castle. (The 34-mile stretch of coast path from St Ives to Penzance is often tackled as a separate expedition, if the walker has only a few days to spare.)

From Penzance the long-distance route hugs the eastern shore of Mount's Bay by beach and shattered headland, by the dramatic Mullion Harbour and the lovely Kynance Cove, and so runs on to the serpentine country of the Lizard and the most southerly point of the mainland of Great Britain.

Rich and colourful vegetation by the coast path above Lizard Point

The Lizard to Plymouth Sound (92 miles)

From Lizard Point to St Anthony Head on the Falmouth Estuary, the Cornwall Coast Path changes character in a remarkable way. The vegetation becomes more lush, the headlands and the charming fishing coves, like Cadgwith and Coverack, are less rugged and more subtly complex in their forms. Two great waterways divide the land at Helford and Carrick Roads, creating enchanting networks of creeks and wooded river banks that cause the walker some problems of navigation.

There are various ferry crossings but these can be seasonal, so the coast path walker should make a careful check beforehand of local details.

Falmouth is a substantial Cornish town only a few miles from the county town of Truro, the very heartland of cultural and commercial Cornwall, seemingly far removed from those great raw-boned cliffs of the north and west. Beyond Falmouth lies the lovely Roseland Peninsula where our route leads on by Gerrans Bay and Nare Head to the great headland of the Dodman, with its magnificent Iron Age ramparts. To the north lie Gorran Haven and Mevagissey, immensely popular with visitors but nevertheless retaining much of their charm in the surviving architecture of the traditional fishing village.

The scene changes to St Austell Bay with its industrial hinterland amidst the white clay 'alps' of Hensbarrow, the bay itself enclosed by Gribben Head, with Fowey to the east at the southern termination of the Saints' Way.

From here the coast path leads on through Polperro and Looe to where the great sweep of Whitsand Bay brings the walker to Rame Head and the delightful Mount Edgcumbe which stands on the shores of Plymouth South – the effective culmination of one of the great coastal walks of the British Isles.

The Tinners' Way (13 miles)

One of several standing stones on the Tinners' Way, on Mên Scryfa Down near Madron

The Tinners' Way is a 13-mile walking route from St Just to St Ives on the Land's End Peninsula.

It is a relatively new concept and is still being defined. Right of access may not exist throughout its length, although the lanes and tracks involved have existed for many years as part of a network of ancient ways across the peninsula.

The Tinners' Way follows a line of a high granite ridgeway that was probably one of the original lines of communication in pre-history, when the bare summit of the ridge stood clear of the densely covered lowland.

There is evidence that the route was used for transporting minerals from the Bronze Age up until the 19th century, a period of almost 4,000 years. It would have been part of a network of tracks connecting seashore ports with the country inland and with their counterparts on the opposite coast.

The modern concept of the Tinners' Way, or 'Forth an Stenoryon' as it is known in Cornish, is an imaginative creation based on what remains of this ancient network of communications. It should be said that archaeologists are sceptical about the route, but it nevertheless makes for a full day's expedition through some of the most magnificent country in Cornwall.

The Tinners' Way starts at Cape Cornwall near St Just. From the car park the route follows the coastal path northwards before turning inland to cross the main north coast road at Truthwall. It leads up on to the high moors, the most ancient of Cornish landscapes, punctuated frequently by the granite monuments of early people, including standing stones, burial chambers, Iron Age castles, ancient villages and stone circles.

For eight miles the Tinners' Way traverses the lonely moors before reaching the delightful little church of Towednack in a valley leading up from the sea. From here, alternative routes can be taken by road, or along the old field paths that lead down to the coast at St Ives.

The Saints' Way

(30 miles approx.)

Cornwall's Saints' Way, or 'Forth an Syns' as it is known in the ancient language, is an imaginative reconstruction sponsored by the CRS Community Programme. It follows one of the cross-country routes travelled by Welsh and Irish 'saints' of the Dark Ages, between AD400 and 700.

It traverses the 'waist' of the county from Padstow on the north coast to Fowey on the south, and throughout its length is waymarked by distinctive Saints' Way signposts.

Relics of St Petroc in Bodmin Church

The Saints' Way is about 30 miles long and runs through a dozen parishes, across landscapes which are vivid and varied and as Cornish as the county's more famous coastline.

The route is linked by significant relics of Cornish history, from the ancient shrines and burial chambers of Neolithic times to the handsome mediaeval churches founded by the Normans and the sterner Wesleyan meeting houses of the 18th century.

The 20th century intrudes but the Saints' Way goes across the grain of the land and modern roads are quickly crossed. The side roads, which in places have supplanted the old byways, are themselves relatively peaceful.

Its religious connections apart, the Saints' Way would have been a traditional trade route linking the north and south coasts of Cornwall. For many centuries Welsh and Irish merchants disembarked at Padstow before crossing overland to Fowey and the shores of St Austell Bay, where they re-embarked for Brittany. It was a journey taken in preference to the sea-passage round Land's End,

Holy well at Luxulyan, one of several wells whose waters were believed to have healing powers

whose savage and storm-battered coast must have had as bad a reputation in ancient times as Cape Horn has today.

The symbolic starting point for the Saints' Way is the south door of Padstow parish church, where, in AD520, the Welsh St Petroc established a small monastic settlement. From here the route goes southwards through Padstow Parish by footpath, lane and field, to the combined parishes of the charmingly named Little Petherick and St Issey.

The influence of St Petroc along this northern part of the Saints' Way is evident, in place names and in religious foundations. The name Petherick is a mediaeval form of Petroc, while the Saint's spirit and influence travel on towards St Breock and Bodmin. From St Breock Downs, superb views can be had to the Camel estuary in the north and to the white clay 'mountains' near St Austell in the south.

From here the Saints' Way continues to the Parish of Withiel, with the great rocks of Helman Tor leading the walker on through Lanivet Parish to the south of Bodmin, until reaching the Helman Tor gate on the bounds of the parish of Lanlivery.

Here the modern Saints' Way divides, one route going via Lanlivery, with its fine church tower, and St Samson's Parish, its church small but full of interest, and on to Fowey; while the other goes via Luxulyan, especially lovely at bluebell time, St Blazey, and Tywardreath, site of a priory founded soon after the Norman Conquest of which nothing remains.

Helman Tor is literally the high point of the Saints' Way. It is truly characteristic of the 'Granite Kingdom' with its great wind-eroded rocks surmounting the hill-top above acres of willow and gorse, the whole area retaining some of the flavour of that ancient country traversed by saint and trader alike.

The eastern route to Fowey via Lanlivery goes through the wooded estuary of the Fowey river, traditional meeting place of Tristan and Iseult. The western route, which is slightly longer, takes in part of an ancient track with handsome granite stiles and cobbled causeway, whose rediscovery in 1984 was the inspiration for the present Saints' Way.

The accepted end to this remarkable journey across Cornwall is the Church of St Finbar at Fowey. Finbar was a 7th-century Irish saint, who travelled via Cornwall to Brittany and Rome and founded a Christian cell at Fowey. Thus for the modern pilgrim the Saints' Way is linked from Padstow to the southern shore.

For more information about these paths, contact Cornwall Tourist Board, Old County Hall, Station Road, Truro TR1 1BR. Tel: (0872) 74282, ext 3101.

Gazetteer

▲ Cotehele House

Each entry in this Gazetteer has the atlas
page number on which the place can be
found and its National Grid reference
included under the heading. An
explanation of how to use the National
Grid is given on page 86.

ALTARNUN
MAP REF: 95SX2281

Sheltering beneath the eastern heights of Bodmin Moor, this attractive village is bisected by a peat-brown stream rushing under a 15th-century packhorse bridge to join the River Tamar. Well-tended gardens stand before granite, slate-hung and colour-washed cottages, and dominating all is the impressive pinnacled tower of the 15th-century church, dedicated to St Nonna (the mother of St David, patron saint of Wales). It is known as 'The Cathedral of the Moor'. Its spacious, light interior, barrel-roof, carved rood-screen and decorated Norman font make it one of the finest West Country churches. Over 70 delightfully carved 16th-century bench-ends are the work of Robert Daye. There is a fascinating inscription along the entire length of the altar rail which offers an intriguing 'word game'. Another great craftsman, the sculptor Nevil Northey Burnard, was born in the village in 1818.

John Wesley visited Altarnun on many occasions while staying at the Isbell Cottage at Trewint, ¼ mile west and just off the A30. The charmingly preserved Isbell Cottage is open to the public. It has a 'Prophet's Room' specially built by Digory Isbell to accommodate Wesley and his fellow preachers. There is an adjoining Pilgrim's Garden.

▲ At one time Bodmin was renowned for its holy wells. This one is St Guron's

BLISLAND
MAP REF: 94SX1073

Reached by twisting lanes on the western slopes of Bodmin Moor, this pretty, well-kept village overlooks the valley of the River Camel. Around the large, tree-lined village green – which retains its original Saxon plan – stand Georgian and Victorian houses and cottages, a manor house, forge, schoolhouse, rectory and old inn, the Royal Oak. The Norman and medieval church, dedicated jointly to St Protus and St Hyacinth and known locally as St Pratts, has a white-walled interior deservedly described as 'dazzling and amazing' by Sir John Betjeman. It has pleasingly uneven columns, a fine wagon roof and an intriguing Renaissance-style altar.

Hawks Tor and the Neolithic stone circle, the Stripple Stones, are 3 miles north-east of Blisland.

BODMIN
MAP REF: 92SX0767

The bustling, narrow streets of this hillside town owe their origins to a Welsh missionary, St Petroc, who settled here in the 6th century. The town grew up around a monastery and priory, and by the time of Domesday Book it was the only town in Cornwall to boast a market. The mighty 15th-century church is the largest in the county and once contained the relics of St Petroc.

Bodmin became a centre for Cornish rebellion, and one of its sons, Thomas Flamank, led an ill-fated march on London in 1497, to protest against taxation.

Winning the Right of Assize in 1835, Bodmin became the county town and its growth was further aided by the arrival of one of the earliest railways in Britain, linking it with the port of Wadebridge. Only with the growth of Truro has Bodmin's role declined, but it remains a town of great character, its Assize Court and Tudor Guildhall being particularly worthy of note. Rising above the town is the 18-acre Beacon with its 144ft obelisk, a memorial to local landowner Sir Walter Raleigh Gilbert. The once-feared Bodmin Jail, scene of many public executions, is now a hotel, and the former headquarters of the Duke of Cornwall's Light Infantry now houses a Regimental Museum. There is also an excellent Bodmin Town Museum, recently refurbished. Bodmin has an indoor tennis and sports centre with three grass courts and an all-weather, multi-purpose

▼ Altarnun's 15th-century packhorse bridge, with St Nonna's in the background

MAP REF: 95SX2075

Less fearsome than neighbouring Dartmoor, the granite uplands of Bodmin Moor are still wild and desolate, topped by brooding tors. The remains of Bronze Age settlements and ancient field systems are scattered across the lower slopes of the spectacular rocky summit of Rough Tor (1,300ft). Beyond this lies Brown Willy (1,377ft) the highest point in Cornwall. Both can be reached by an exhilarating walk from the car park at the end of the road which leads south-west from Camelford for 2 miles. Rough Tor is an official war memorial to the Wessex Regiment.

At the moor's centre, on the main A30, stands Jamaica Inn. This slate-hung 18th-century building was a welcome stop for smugglers carrying illicit cargoes. On the lonely moorland to the south is Dozmary Pool where, according to legend, King Arthur's sword Excalibur was received by a hand rising from the water.

sports pitch. The Bodmin Steam Railway offers a nostalgic journey through the beautiful Glynn Valley.

▲ Looking across the uplands of Bodmin Moor, an expanse of 80 square miles of rough grazing, peaking at Rough Tor

WRITERS

The names of many writers are inextricably linked with Cornwall, none more so than that of Bodmin-born author and literary critic, Sir Arthur Quiller-Couch. Under the pseudonym of 'Q' he wrote lovingly about Cornwall and Fowey, his home for 50 years, which appears as 'Troy Town' in his novels. The writer Kenneth Grahame, author of *The Wind in the Willows* and a friend of 'Q', paid many visits to Fowey.

Cornwall's china clay country has produced two distinguished writers: the poet and novelist Jack Clemo, deaf and blind for most of his writing career, and the historian, poet and leading authority on the Elizabethan Age, Dr A L Rowse. Another celebrated poet, Charles Causley, still lives in Launceston, while at Carnkie in the shadow of Carn Brea, the poet and author of *The White Hotel*, D M Thomas, was born.

Many writers born east of the Tamar have also sought inspiration in Cornwall, and the Valency Valley will forever be linked with Thomas Hardy and his first wife Emma, whom he met while restoring St Juliot church. The high north coast cliffs and lush inland valleys are strikingly invoked in his novel *A Pair of Blue Eyes*. D H Lawrence wrote much of *Women in Love* while living in a cottage

surrounded by Iron Age fields in Zennor in the early years of World War I. Lawrence's carelessness about blackout regulations led to local suspicion that flickering lights in his cottage window were relaying semaphore to German submarines. Lawrence and his German wife Freida were eventually hounded out of Cornwall; a trauma reproduced in the 'nightmare' sequence of Lawrence's novel *Kangaroo*. Dylan Thomas and his wife Caitlin lived for a while at Mousehole, which Thomas described as 'really the loveliest village in England'. It is possible that the fishing village of Llaregyb in *Under Milk Wood* owes as much to Mousehole as to his home village of Laugharne in Wales.

Virginia Woolf's childhood holidays in St Ives and picnics near Godrevy provided the background setting for her novel *To the Lighthouse*. Cornwall also provided the background for the most famous novels by Daphne du Maurier. *House on the Strand* is based in Tywardreath, near St Austell, while the famous 'Manderley' in *Rebecca* is based on Menabilly, west of Fowey, where she lived for a while. When Daphne du Maurier stayed at Jamaica Inn on Bodmin Moor between the wars and wrote her tale of Mary Yellan, Joss Merlin and his smuggling activities, it was

▲ A portrait of D H Lawrence whose novel *Women in Love* was written while he was living in Zennor

in fact a Temperance Hotel.

The area around Polzeath is renowned as John Betjeman Country, for here he spent happy childhood holidays. He later wove its villages, lanes, churches, coastline and golf-courses into his evocative poems. Further west, around Perranporth and St Agnes, we are in Poldark country, the setting for Winston Graham's ten *Poldark* novels depicting life in a late 18th-century mining community. More recently, the novelist E V Thompson chose the heights of Bodmin Moor and several south coast ports as the locations for his books *Chase the Wind* and *Ben Retallick*.

▲ Boscastle harbour, surrounded by steep slate cliffs

railway superceded canal transport. There is a canalside museum. Bude was developed as a family resort in Victorian and Edwardian times. The treacherous cliffs of Cornwall's north coast here give way to wide sandy beaches, backed by grassy downland and sandhills. The small castle on a mound by the canal entrance was built in 1850 by Sir Goldworthy Gurney. About a mile inland the small market town of Stratton was the birthplace of Anthony Payne, the 'Cornish Giant'. Born in the Tree Inn he stood over 7ft tall and fought beside his master, Sir Bevill Grenville, at the nearby Battle of Stamford Hill in 1643.

Bude's Summerleaze Beach is exhilarating and spacious with acres of sand when the tide is out. Crooklets Beach just to the north is an excellent surfing venue while the mile-long Widemouth Bay 2½ miles to the south of Bude is ideal for both families and surfers. The Bude Surf Life Saving Club, formed in 1953, was the first in Britain.

BOSCASTLE
MAP REF: 94SX0990

The narrow ravine-like entrance to Boscastle harbour – little more than a cleft in the slate cliffs – leads to a long heather-clad valley and a tiny 16th-century pier from which slate and corn were exported. There are some charming old buildings in Boscastle including two splendid examples in Fore Street, one called 'Smugglers' and the other 'Tinkers'. Higher up the combe, lime-washed cottages cluster round the water-mill at the foot of the pretty hillside village. During the Napoleonic Wars soldiers were recruited in two old coaching inns, the Wellington and the Napoleon. On the opposite hillside a few stones are all that remain of Bottreaux castle, once held by the Breton de Botterell family, which gave the village its name. An unusual Museum of Witchcraft contains many sinister artefacts. The National Trust owns much of the land round Boscastle and its harbour. There is an information centre at The Old Forge on the harbourside. The novelist Thomas Hardy often visited Boscastle when he was a young architect, restoring the hillside Church of St Juliot. He courted and married the rector's sister-in-law, Emma, and many of his poems and the novel *A Pair of Blue Eyes* describe the area. A riverside walk leads up the valley of the River Valency to St Juliot Church at Hennett and back along the south side of the valley, passing the churches of Lesnewth and Minster.

BREAGE
MAP REF: 90SW6128

The old church of St Breaca at the centre of this small farming community contains a series of bold wall-paintings, discovered last century under a layer of lime-wash. Painted in the 15th century by peripatetic monastic artists, they depict St Christopher and Christ blessing the Trades.

The handsome Godolphin Hall lies 2¼ miles north of Breage. It is open to the public on certain days only. Part early 16th-century with substantial 17th-century additions, the Hall was home of the Godolphin family, prominent Elizabethans and Royalists. The north side of the Hall comprises a charming loggia with seven bays and very un-Cornish Tuscan columns.

On the coast, 1½ miles south-west of Germoe is Prussia Cove, named after the famous 18th-century smuggler John Carter who styled himself after Frederick the Great of Prussia.

BUDE
MAP REF: 95SS2106

Once a busy port, from which cargoes of sand and seaweed were carried along a canal to Launceston for fertiliser.

The Bude Canal was initially planned to link the Bristol Channel with the English Channel via Launceston and the River Tamar. However, the full scheme never materialised and the coming of the

CADGWITH
MAP REF: 91SW7214

Sheltering east of the Lizard, Cadgwith is a small, picturesque fishing community of pink and whitewashed cottages, their thatch held down against winter gales by heavy chains. A rocky promontory, the Todden, divides two steep shingle beaches up which fishing boats are hauled over wooden rollers by a winch. Today the chief catches are crab, lobster and mixed fish, including pollack, ling and conger. In the 19th century Cadgwith held the record for catching pilchards – 1,300,000 in a single day. The old pilchard cellar, where the fish were packed in barrels, stands next to the

▼ A 15th-century wall painting of Christ blessing the Trades, in the church of St Breaca at Breage

▲ The harbour at Bude and the entrance to the canal to Launceston

old inn where fishermen's voices are often raised in salty song.

On the headland to the east of Cadgwith Beach is a small, dark building with a tall chimney. This was a coastguard watchhouse built late last century. Prior to this there was a strong contingent of customs or 'Preventive' men permanently stationed at Cadgwith to police this notorious smuggling coast; with little success of course.

Along the springy clifftop to the south is a collapsed sea-cave known as the Devil's Frying Pan. There is a circular nature trail through the Poltesco valley. This takes in the remains of an old serpentine works at Carleon Cove to the north of

Cadgwith. The Lizard area is famed for the ornamental working of serpentine and the factory at Carleon was established in the 1850s. Finished articles were ferried out from the cove in barges to trading ships in the bay. The factory closed in the 1890s.

CALLINGTON
MAP REF: 93SX3669

This small market town of slate-hung houses stands on high land between the valleys of the rivers Lynher and Tamar, surrounded by lush fruit-growing country. Meandering lanes lead past orchards and market gardens to the secluded village of St Dominick with its 13th-century church. Callington was at the heart of a Victorian industrial area that straddled the Cornwall-Devon border. Copper mines were plentiful, not least on the impressive Kit Hill which rises to just over 1,000ft to the north-east of the town. The hill is a treasure-house of industrial archaeology, its summit crowned by a massive 80ft-high stack built in 1858. The 500-acre Kit Hill was given to Cornwall by Prince Charles, the Duke of Cornwall in 1985 and is now a Country Park. There are unrivalled views from the summit, ample parking, and a circular walk and industrial heritage trail add to the interest.

CALSTOCK
MAP REF: 93SX4368

The 12 graceful arches of the railway viaduct tower over the town of Calstock, sprawling along the steep northern bank of the River Tamar. The viaduct was completed in 1908. It was built entirely of concrete blocks and its graceful lines say much about the triumph of design over raw material. Calstock is wedded entirely to the River Tamar. It was the coming of the railway that caused the decline of Calstock's Victorian glory. In its great days, Tamar barges, schooners, ketches and steam coasters dominated the river. They carried copper, tin and granite from local mines and quarries, fruit and produce from extensive market gardens, and brought limestone and other goods and raw materials to the town. Paddle-steamers operated on the river and Calstock boasted a thriving boat-building industry.

St Andrew's Church is gained by a stiff walk up Church Hill from Calstock village. Some early 14th-century pillars remain, but the church was restored unsympathetically in 1867 under the heavy hand of James Piers St Aubyn. The views from the churchyard are impressive. Inside the church are memorials to the Edgcumbe family whose home, Cotehele, lies around a bend in the river.

▼ Lobster and crab are the main catch of Cadgwith's fishermen today

▲ The engine-house of the whim beam engine near Camborne

CAMBORNE
MAP REF: 90SW6440

The area surrounding Camborne and Redruth was once the most intensely mined in the world. In the 1850s two-thirds of the world's copper was produced by nearly 350 mines employing 50,000 underground workers. The deepest mine was Dolcoath (3,000ft deep), but like most of the others it closed early this century when cheaper deposits of tin and copper were discovered overseas. Miners and their families were forced to emigrate to America, Australia and South Africa.

The historical importance of the Camborne area is being increasingly recognised and efforts are being made to have the mining area included on the United Nations list of World Heritage Sites. The engineer Richard Trevithick was born at Penponds in 1771. His statue stands in front of the town's library and he is joyfully remembered each April when a colourful Trevithick Day procession is held in the town. The cottage in which Trevithick spent his early years at Penponds is maintained by the National Trust.

Modern Camborne is a busy shopping centre with light industry flourishing at its outskirts. Several fine Wesleyan chapels bear witness to the success of Methodism among mining communities, and at the town's centre stands the 15th-century parish church of St Meriadocus.

At Pool, to the north, are the East Pool Cornish Beam Engines; working, pumping and winding engines owned by the National Trust. A colourful display of rock and mineral specimens can be seen at the School of Mines Museum, and close by is Carn Brea Leisure Centre.

▲ Exhibits in the museum at Camelford

CAMELFORD
MAP REF: 94SX1083

The humped camel decorating the weathervane on the town hall is misleading, for the town's name probably stems from the Cornish words *cam pol* or 'winding river', an apt description. Slate predominates in this old wool town and former pocket borough. A coach-house has been converted into the excellent North Cornwall Museum and Gallery where folk items and a fully furnished cottage interior are displayed. A road leads east to Crowdy Reservoir, where anglers can try their luck fishing for brown and rainbow trout, and continues to a car park from where a walk can be taken to the rocky outcrop of Rough Tor. Just over a mile north of Camelford is the ominously named Slaughterbridge, the site of a 9th-century battle where the legendary King Arthur is said to have been killed. A stone marks the site.

INVENTORS

Towards the end of April each year, the flag-hung streets of Camborne are crowded with people and steam-powered traction engines in honour of the local engineering genius and 'Father of the Locomotive', Richard Trevithick. Born in 1771, Trevithick unquestionably did more for the development of the steam engine than anyone else, including the better-known James Watt and George Stephenson, and ran his first steam road-carriage in 1802. Half-way up a hill it ran out of steam and rolled back to the bottom, an occasion recalled in a favourite local song, *Going up Camborne Hill, Coming Down*. Trevithick built a second more powerful locomotive and took it to London. Called the *Catch-me-who-can*, it carried passengers on a circular track at 15mph. In 1804 he took another engine to Wales, where it hauled ten wagons of coal, each weighing ten tons. This was 20 years before Stephenson's first successful running of *Locomotive One*.

The high-pressure steam pumping engines developed by Trevithick, Newcomen and West allowed mines to be kept relatively water-free and miners to drill to much deeper levels. The lack of national fame accorded Richard Trevithick is probably due to his tendency to spread his genius thinly over a wide range of projects. As well as devising a Thames tunnel and a tower taller than Eiffel's, he also invented a steam-powered lift, dredger and threshing machine. A statue to the great man stands in front of Camborne public library.

Another great pioneer of steam-power, Goldsworthy Gurney, was inspired as a youngster by Trevithick's machines. Born at Padstow in 1793, in 1823 he experimented using steam boilers to power road vehicles that 'resembled common stage coaches, but without horses'. A year later he succeeded in carrying 18 passengers, six inside and 12 on top of the carriage, from Bath to London at 15mph. A regular service of Gurney coaches linked Gloucester with Cheltenham in 1831. Gurney's other achievements included an oxy-hydrogen blow pipe for quenching fires in mines, the 'Gurney Stove', used to heat the House of Commons, and a mock castle built on sand at Bude. Goldsworthy Gurney was knighted in 1863 and died 12 years later.

At the head of Market Jew Street in Penzance, stands a statue honouring the scientist and inventor, Sir Humphry Davy. Best known as the inventor of the miners' safety lamp, Davy also conducted pioneering research into gases. One of these, nitrous oxide or 'laughing gas', was later to be used as an anaesthetic. However, Davy's greatest achievement was probably his work on electrolysis. He isolated and named sodium and potassium, the gases chlorine and fluorine and the metals barium, strontium and calcium.

CAWSAND AND KINGSAND

MAP REF: 93SX4350

These 'twin' villages lie on Rame Head Peninsula overlooking Plymouth Sound. They have a particular charm; retaining their individual characters yet merging imperceptibly. Locals know where the join is however since the tiny stream that divides the two was the ancient border between Celtic Cornwall and Saxon England. There were close links with Brittany and the proximity of Plymouth meant a lucrative smuggling trade in luxury goods like spirits and silk. In 1804 it was estimated that 17,000 casks of spirits were smuggled through the two villages each year.

There are fine coastal walks in the area with extensive views of Plymouth Sound and its famous Breakwater, which was finally completed in 1841 after 30 years of work. A stroll through the narrow winding lanes of Cawsand and Kingsand is a pleasure. There are small shingle beaches and a handsome clock-tower on the shoreline. There is excellent parking at Cawsand.

CHARLESTOWN

MAP REF: 92SX0351

Charlestown was originally known as Polmear Cove. In the mid-18th century it was simply a small beach with one or two pilchard boats and a handful of cottages. The present port was literally dug out from the land by local landowner and mining adventurer Charles Rashleigh. Completed in 1801, the initial use

▲ The beautifully preserved grey granite buildings at Cotehele

was for exporting copper ore from nearby mines, but china clay soon became the main export with coal the main import. Local workers fell into one of two categories: those with clay-white faces and clothes and those covered with coal-dust.

Charlestown also boasted a shipyard, ropewalk, warehouses, limekiln, brickworks and even a pilchard fishery. The harbour wharfs and lock-gates were designed by the engineer John Smeaton, and the entire town, including workers houses, was carefully planned at one stroke, with a broad tree-lined, main street running down to the harbour. The unspoilt charm of Charlestown led to it becoming popular as a film

location; *Poldark, The Onedin Line, The Voyage of Charles Darwin* and *The Eagle has Landed* all being partly filmed here. A portrayal of 19th-century life in the port can be seen in Charlestown Shipwreck and Heritage Museum. Along the coast to the east is the broad sandy beach of Carlyon Bay, the Cornish Leisure World and the Cornwall Coliseum.

COTEHELE

MAP REF: 93SX4268

The grey granite home of the Edgcumbe family overlooking the Tamar valley, is now in the care of the National Trust. It is reached from the A390 just west of Gunnislake. In 1553 the family moved to Mount Edgcumbe, 10 miles to the south, and Cotehele was subsequently only occasionally occupied. The Tudor home has remained virtually unaltered since the addition of a tower in 1627, and most of the original furnishings are intact. Well-tended gardens and banks of rhododendrons surround a restored mediaeval dovecote, and a path winds down through dense woodland to the riverside.

Alongside the River Tamar at Cotehele Quay, is a small museum, a splendidly-restored boathouse and *Shamrock*, one of the last sailing-barges to carry stone down the river. A short woodland walk leads to a watermill, a cider press, forge and wheelwright's shop.

◄ Charlestown harbour, built in 1801 for trade in coal and china clay

COVERACK
MAP REF: 91SW7818

Sheltered by the Lizard from fierce south-westerly gales, there has been a community here since medieval times with pilchard fishing being the main occupation until early this century. Over the years its lifeboat crew performed many heroic deeds, rescuing mariners and vessels wrecked on the dreaded Manacles Rocks further along the coast. The Paris Inn at Coverack was named after the liner SS *Paris* that ran aground on the nearby coast in May 1899 and was safely refloated. Coverack was formerly known for its smuggling activities and several of

limestone and exporting locally quarried slate. Donkeys and horses were used to carry tons of sand and seaweed from Crackington Beach for use as fertiliser, while shingle and stone were taken for building.

An energetic walk south leads to High Cliff, 730ft above The Strangles beach. Crackington has given its name to the fantastically twisted rock formations on the cliffs. Known as the 'Crackington Measures' they are visually striking but extremely loose. The cliffs should not be approached too closely.

The hamlet of St Gennys (pronounced with a hard 'g') to the north commands wide coastal views as far as Hartland Point.

▲ The beach at Crackington Haven

infected the region which became a kind of Cornish Sodom and Gomorrah. A three day tempest of blown sand buried Langarroc for ever. Substance was given to the legend when local farmers ploughed up numerous teeth and bones from the sandy soil.

Over the dunes is Crantock Beach, and to the south are the surfing beaches of Porth Joke and Holywell Bay.

CREMYLL
MAP REF: 93SX4553

Cremyll is an historic passenger ferry point on the Cornish shores of Plymouth Sound. The ferry trip from Plymouth is a splendid way of entering Cornwall – on foot! Cremyll has been a boat-building centre for many years and is internationally known amongst yachtsmen for the

▼ The harbour at Falmouth, which was once Britain's second busiest port

▲ The little sheltered harbour at Coverack, until this century the scene of a healthy pilchard fishing industry

the cottages have secret hiding-places under their stone floors.

Chynhalls Point, an Iron Age cliff castle lies 1/2 mile to the south and is worth visiting. A mile further south is the notorious Black Head with its 230ft of wrecking cliff rising from the sea.

CRACKINGTON HAVEN
MAP REF: 95SX1496

A long, peaceful, gorse-clad valley owned by the National Trust opens out on to a sandy beach washed by high, and sometimes dangerous, surf. Sheltered by towering cliffs, the beach was formerly used as a small port for unloading Welsh coal and

CRANTOCK
MAP REF: 91SW7960

This ancient village of colour-washed cottages and pretty gardens is separated from the bustle of Newquay by a long, narrow estuary, The Gannel. The village stocks, last used in 1817 to punish a smuggler, stand outside the 5th-century St Carantocus church. The thatched Old Albion Inn contains a secret chamber, used by smugglers, under its stone floor.

The legendary city of Langarroc once stretched far down the coast to the south. Its wealthy citizens grew indolent and employed convicts to work for them. Lawlessness soon

excellence of its shipwright's work. There is a waterfront pub at Cremyll overlooking Plymouth Sound. Nearby is Mount Edgecumbe Country Park. Landscaped gardens, including an English, Italian and French enclosure and fallow deer are just a few of the delights of the immediate parkland where the visitor may follow in the footsteps of numerous monarchs and two famous Samuels – Johnson and Pepys.

DELABOLE
MAP REF: 94SX0784

Slate quarrying has been carried out in this area since Elizabethan times and possibly much earlier. Delabole Slate Quarry is the largest man-made hole in Britain, and 500 men were once employed here; blasting, cutting and splitting the blue-grey slate. Cheaper substitutes have caused a decline in the industry. The public is not allowed into the quarry, but a viewing area affords a dizzying view of the quarry below and there is a showroom and exhibition.

FALMOUTH
MAP REF: 91SW8032

Its position at the entrance to a large stretch of deep, sheltered water – the estuary of seven rivers – made Falmouth ideal for development as a defendable port. Before Tudor times it was a small fishing village known as Penny-come-quick, but the enthusiasm of Sir Walter Raleigh and the foresight of the local piratical Killigrew family, caused quick growth in the late 16th century. Pendennis Castle and its smaller neighbour across the water, St Mawes, were built on either side of the entrance to Carrick Roads to defend the port against invaders.

Falmouth became known as 'the Front Porch of Britain', being an ideal place to replenish supplies for inbound ships and suitably sheltered for outward-bound vessels awaiting favourable winds. For 200 years Falmouth was the base for the 'Packet Service' sailing ships. In 1827 about 40 packet ships were based at Falmouth but the introduction of steam signalled their decline, with Southampton taking over as the Packet port by 1850. The arrival of the railway in 1863 brought renewed affluence, and the south-facing side of the town was developed as a holiday resort.

There has been extensive infilling and waterside development at Falmouth in recent years and today the port is a popular yachting centre, earning prosperity from tourism, shipping and ship-repairing. On many summer evenings Falmouth's gaff-rigged working boats race offshore. They evolved from the quay punts which would race out to incoming sailing vessels to claim tendering rights during their stay. Similar small vessels still dredge under sail for oysters in the estuary. At the town's centre is the Prince of Wales Pier from where pleasure trips can be taken or the ferry caught to Flushing or St Mawes. Close by is a tree-lined open space known as The Moor. The town hall houses the art gallery, and on the opposite side is a precipitous flight of 111 steps known as 'Jacob's Ladder'. Alongside the Custom House is a chimney known as the 'Queen's Pipe' where contraband tobacco was burnt, and a tiny harbour which has witnessed the arrival and departure of many record-breaking voyages. The Falmouth Maritime Museum is in Bell's Court. At the southern end of the main street is Arwenack, the 17th-century manor house of the Killigrew family who developed the port.

▲ This circular-headed Celtic cross stands in Feock churchyard

FEOCK
MAP REF: 91SW8238

This creekside village overlooks the Carrick Roads, the third-largest deep water anchorage in the world. Ocean-going cargo ships and even oil platforms are often laid up at anchor in the 'Roads'. Feock consists of a cluster of whitewashed and thatched cottages and a number of modern, affluent properties. Its small church nestling in a green bowl of yew trees has a separate 13th-century tower and an interesting lych-gate with a slate-hung upper storey. A lane descends steeply to shingly Loe Beach where vessels of all sizes and shapes take to the safe waters of Carrick Roads. To the south the long arm of Restronguet Point reaches out across the mouth of a creek. From its tip a ferry runs the short distance to Restronguet Passage. This was on the main post route from Falmouth to Truro during the 19th century. The charming Pandora Inn beckons from the Mylor side. A peaceful creekside walk from Feock follows the old tram-road from Penpol to Devoran through what was a major industrial area in Victorian times.

▲ Looking over the Gothic tower of Place House, Fowey, towards Polruan

FLUSHING

MAP REF: 91SW8033

Said to have the mildest climate in Britain, the trim little village and quay of Flushing faces Falmouth across the narrow Penryn River. There is a passenger ferry to Falmouth. Flushing owes its name to 17th-century Dutch builders from Holland who settled here. The village retains a distinctly Dutch atmosphere. A lane winding up between delightful gardens leads to a small park and vantage point over the village rooftops. Just north of Flushing is Little Falmouth where many of the 19th-century mail delivery ships, the famous Falmouth Packets, were built.

FOWEY

MAP REF: 92SX1251

An historic town overlooking a deep-water anchorage, Fowey (pronounced 'Foy') is one of Cornwall's most picturesque and romantic places. The pace of life in its narrow streets is easy and there are few concessions to modern 'development'. Fowey's buildings are delightful, and range in architectural style from Elizabethan to Edwardian. The shipping of tin ore from here to France was halted by the Hundred Years War when over 700 local seamen were recruited to sail against the French. Known as the 'Fowey Gallants', many were later to become much-feared pirates, raiding any ship that strayed into Cornish waters. After the French ransacked the town in 1457, blockhouses were built on either side of the entrance to Fowey harbour and a chain stretched between them to de-mast any

invading ships. To strengthen the defences further, Henry VIII built one of his many castles along this coast at Readymoney Cove. Many Edwardian visitors were attracted to the town by the writings of Sir Arthur Quiller-Couch, the famous 'Q', in which Fowey was thinly disguised as 'Troy Town'. His home stands below the Esplanade overlooking the boat-filled river. The rail link with Lostwithiel in 1864 and the great depth of the river has enabled Fowey to become one of Cornwall's leading china clay exporters; freighters of 10,000 tons nosing their way through pleasure craft to the clay wharfs north of the town.

Walk along the high narrow lane of Bull Hill for a panoramic rooftop view of the town and river, or follow the winding length of Fore Street to visit the Noah's Ark Museum. An exhibition describing the town's history can be found in the Town Hall Museum in Fowey's Trafalgar Square. The Ship Inn, once the home of the Rashleigh family, boasts some fine Elizabethan panelling and plaster ceilings. The romantic neo-Gothic building towering over the town is Place House, the seat of the Treffry family. Dating from the 15th century, but largely rebuilt in the 1840s, it is only occasionally open to the public. The Bodinnick car ferry crosses the river at Caffamill Pill and a passenger ferry weaves through a flotilla of yachts to the small port and hillside village of Polruan on the opposite bank. There is a Royal Regatta and Carnival at Fowey in August.

A few miles up-river from Fowey is Golant, a cluster of riverside cottages with the 16th-century St Sampson's

church containing a pulpit made from old carved bench-ends. This area has strong links with the tragic lovers Tristan and Iseult. Tristan's father, King Mark of Cornwall, is said to have lived at Castle Dore, a circular earthwork to the west of the village.

FOOD

Tes plain and nothin' fancy, but it do stick to your ribs,' was how one St Just housewife described Cornish food. She might have added 'full of variety', for everything is grist to the Cornish cook's mill. The pie was for many years the medium through which her art was revealed: pilchard pie, mackerel pie, bream pie, conger pie, curlew pie, giblet pie and ram pie all being popular dishes. Squab pie contained young pigeons; Nattlin pie, pig's entrails; Likky pie, leeks; and Muggety pie was made with sheep's entrails. Starry-gazy pie contained pilchards with their heads poking out through the crust. It is hardly surprising that the devil never came to Cornwall for fear of being put in a pie.

The ubiquitous Cornish pasty bought from a shop or supermarket bears little resemblance to the crimped foot-long home-made concoction enjoyed by farm-workers in the fields or miners deep underground for their 'croust'. Often marked with the consumer's initial in pastry, the pasty was an early convenience food, being held in one hand and eaten from the end.

GRAMPOUND
MAP REF: 91SW9348

Rushing through this modest village on the main A390 road, it is difficult to believe that it was once an ancient borough of great importance. Originally the lowest bridging point on the River Fal, it was a busy market town in the centre of a rich agricultural parish, sending two MPs to Parliament in Elizabethan times as a classic 'Rotten Borough'. Bribery and corruption were rife and the town was denied representation in 1820. Its steep main street still contains several interesting buildings, notably a toll-house by the bridge, a guildhall and clock-tower and a tannery where traditional bark-tanning methods are still used.

◄ The Inn at Ferry Quay, Bodinnick, Fowey

GULVAL
MAP REF: 90SW4831

A charming village of Victorian houses and cottages, compactly grouped round the delightfully situated 15th-century church, Gulval lies on a south-facing slope bright with flowers just a short distance from Penzance. A few miles inland (take the St Ives road and branch left at Badger's Cross) is the Late Iron Age settlement of Chysauster, probably one of the oldest 'villages' in Britain and of a type confined to West Cornwall. Nine courtyard houses, one of which is a semi-detached unit, are grouped on either side of a village street. Dating from the first century BC and abandoned four centuries later, each building consists of a courtyard surrounded by a series of small rooms (stables, living quarters, stores, etc.), each of which would originally have been roofed with thatch. Each house has a small terraced garden-plot, presumably for the growing of herbs and vegetables. Nearby is a fogou, a long, walled ditch which was originally roofed and was used for religious or storage purposes.

▲ The neat, compact Victorian cottages in the small, quiet village of Gulval

The genuine article, made from shortcrust pastry, contains chunks of the best steak (not minced meat), potatoes, onion, turnip, salt and plenty of pepper, but the contents vary from one family to another and remain the subject of endless debate. In stark contrast Cornish fishermen consider it extreme bad luck to take a pasty to sea. This is linked to other 'unlucky' objects and creatures which are seen as being land-based and therefore the antithesis of sea-going. Fishermen will convince you however that a pasty at sea is acceptable so long as the ends have been knocked off, to allow 'the wind to blow through it'!

Cakes and puddings also form an integral part of 'croust' as well as 'high-tea'. Heavy cake (not as indigestible as it sounds) is composed of flour, butter, cream, sugar and currants, rolled out flat and scored with a fish-net pattern. Tatie cake is made from mashed potatoes, fat, flour, currants and sugar while Figgy pudding is made from raisins ('figs') baked with suet, flour, eggs and sugar.

Traditional tea-treats, still held in most villages, culminate in communal hymn-singing and the eating of Saffron buns – yeast buns coloured yellow with saffron from the crocus flower and dotted with currants. Always fond of a 'dish of tay' (cup of tea) many Cornish people stave off the winter cold with something a little stronger. Shenagrum is a warming mixture of rum, brown sugar and a slice of lemon in hot beer, and Mahogany is gin beaten with treacle. Metheglin or mead, made from fermented honey, is also enjoyed in some parts of west Cornwall. Clotted cream is a basic ingredient of any true Cornish tea and no slice of blackberry or apple tart would be quite the same without its dollop of cream. At one time almost every cottage or farm-kitchen had a bowl of golden-encrusted clotted cream cooking slowly on the range. Tubs of locally-made cream retain the home-made quality while having a much longer 'larder-life'. With a butterfat content of 60 per cent, it is slightly thinner than Devon cream and is easier to spread.

▼ Saffron buns at a traditional tea

GUNNISLAKE
MAP REF: 95SX4371

The graceful seven-arched New Bridge, built in 1520, made Gunnislake the lowest crossing point on the River Tamar until modern times. The bridge was the scene of a bloody battle during the 17th-century Civil War. Sir Richard Grenville defended the bridge for the Royalists against the Parliamentarians under Lord Essex. The Parliamentarian army finally took the bridge with the loss of 40 men. The Royalists lost 200. Gunnislake was also the upper tidal reach of the river and locally-mined copper, tin, wolfram and arsenic were shipped downstream from here and Calstock until the early 1900s. Narrow streets of miners' cottages rise steeply up the hillside, and from the top of the main street you can see numerous ruined mine-chimneys and look over the Tamar Valley to the dramatic Morwell Rocks.

From 1800 to World War I the Gunnislake district was served by the 600ft-long Tamar Manure Navigation canal. It was part of a grandiose scheme for linking the Bristol and English Channels, via Launceston and Bude, which never materialised.

GUNWALLOE FISHING COVE

MAP REF: 90SW6522

Little more than a scattering of fishermen's cottages, Gunwalloe Fishing Cove lies at the eastern tip of Mount's Bay. A short walk south takes you to Gunwalloe Church Cove where the small Church of St Winwalloe sits in the dunes beside the beach, surrounded by a hedge of tamarisk. Together with its separate bell-tower, the church appears to be in constant danger of being swept away by waves during storms. The King of Portugal's treasure ship the *St Anthony* was wrecked in Church Cove in 1527. In 1780 a Spanish ship was wrecked in what is now known as Dollar Cove, just north of Church Cove. Several tons of silver dollars were scattered on the tide, many being efficiently salvaged by local people. Rumours of dollars still turning up after storms maintain an enduring but frustrating attraction. It was from the high grassy headland of Poldhu Point to the south that Marconi transmitted the first trans-Atlantic radio signals in 1901.

GWEEK

MAP REF: 91SW7026

At the head of the beautiful Helford River, this peaceful little village with its two bridges was once a busy port, taking over Helston's trade when that town became cut off from the sea. As Penryn, Truro and Falmouth grew, so Gweek's trade declined and the river slowly became choked with silt. The last cargo was carried from its wharfs in 1880, and today its waterfront is a popular place for family boating. Set in pleasant woodland and sloping fields on the north bank is the Cornish Seal Sanctuary, where injured seals are cared for after being washed in on the north coast beaches.

▼ The Seal Sanctuary at Gweek

▲ Looking over the roofs of Gwithian to the church of St Gothian

GWITHIAN

MAP REF: 90SW5841

Backed by high 'towans' or sand-dunes, the three-mile stretch of sand on the eastern side of St Ives Bay offers plenty of space for holidaymakers, even in high summer. The area has become a major venue for wind-surfing and is a favoured site for championship competitions especially in the spectacular 'wave-jumping' events. The village of Gwithian at the northern end contains some charming thatched cottages, a tiny Methodist chapel, an inn and farmhouses. The church is dedicated to St Gothian, an Irish missionary whose monastic cell was unearthed nearby during the last century, but which has now once again been engulfed by sand. Offshore from a high turfy headland owned by the National Trust stands Godrevy lighthouse which formed the haunting image in Virginia Woolf's novel *To The Lighthouse*.

HAYLE

MAP REF: 90SW5637

The name Hayle comes from the Cornish *hayl*, meaning estuary. The full glory of Hayle's seaward prospect, flanked on either side by miles of golden sand, is hidden by the extensive area of old wharf and channels between the town and the sea. The town's historical importance in terms of Victorian industry is immense although industrial decline is evident. However, the harbour area is scheduled for massive residential, recreational and commercial development.

Hayle sprang to prominence last century when its foundries manufactured the boilers, machinery and engines for use in Cornish mines. Richard Trevithick, the great Cornish engineer, built his first steam-powered 'road-carriage' here in the early 1800s, and one of the first railways in the world ran from Hayle to Redruth. Tin and copper were smelted at Copperhouse to the north-east, where a large pool is formed by lock-gates across a stream. There are several fine Victorian buildings in Hayle and the town is enhanced by open areas like the Millpool Gardens and the King George V Memorial Walk, flanking the landlocked Copperhouse Pool. At Paradise Park, south of the town, rare birds and endangered animals can be seen. Brightly-coloured parrots fly free and here also is the red-billed Cornish chough, once a familiar sight around the coast but now locally extinct. Nearby is Phillack with its handsome church and its pub, named the 'Bucket of Blood' centuries ago after a murder victim was found in the brewer's well!

HELFORD

MAP REF: 91SW7526

The peaceful, wood-fringed Helford River, with its deep, sheltered creeks and winding inlets, is one of the most attractive areas of Cornwall. The snug village of Helford, on the south bank, straggles beside a tidal creek and boasts a thatched inn. A ferry from the point beyond the inn goes across the river to Helford Passage and another hostelry of character, the Ferry Boat Inn. West of Helford, and best seen by boat, is Frenchman's Creek, a smuggler's hideaway made

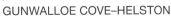
◀ Colour-washed cottages in Helford

delightful walk leads around the borders of the lake which is in the care of the National Trust. Edward I selected Helston as one of Cornwall's stannary towns, where the quality of locally-produced tin was tested ('assayed'), and the wide, sloping main thoroughfare is called Coinagehall Street. The town contains many modest Regency and Georgian buildings and its dipping, winding streets have a genteel quality all their own. The 16th-century Angel Hotel stands below a classic Victorian guildhall, beside which steps lead down to the Butter Market Folk Museum, crammed with interesting items. Across the valley rises the tower of the parish church, destroyed by lightning in 1727 and rebuilt in 1830. In the churchyard is a memorial to Henry Trengrouse, inventor of the rocket apparatus used to save so many lives around the coast. A thatched cottage in Wendron Street is where 'Battling' Bob Fitzsimmons, the only Englishman to become world heavyweight boxing champion, was born. The Blue Anchor Inn, a resting place for monks in the 1400s stands at the lower end of the main street. On market day (Monday) Coinagehall Street is lined with colourful stalls.

South of Helston is The Royal Navy's Air Station at Culdrose, the largest helicopter base in Europe. Here, Sea King helicopter pilots are trained. Culdrose's air-sea rescue record is formidable, with many spectacular sea and cliff rescues to its credit. There is a public viewing area by the car park.

One of Cornwall's leading tourist attractions, Cornwall Aero Park and Flambards Village, can be found close by. This large all-weather attraction features displays of aircraft and helicopters, wartime exhibitions and a Concorde flight-deck. 'Flambards Village' is a splendidly evocative recreation of streets, shops and domestic interiors dating from the turn-of-the-century, while 'Britain in the Blitz' features a wartime street complete with shops, pub and living room with its Morrison shelter. Surrounding all are landscaped gardens, lakes and children's rides and games. North of Helston, near the former mining village of Wendron, is another important tourist attraction, Poldark Mine. Here you can explore the workings underground and experience conditions first-hand. Above ground is a working beam-engine and a fine collection of mining artefacts as well as a children's play-park with rides and games.

▲ Flora Day dancers give spring the traditional Cornish welcome

famous by Daphne du Maurier's novel of that name.

Steep lanes of sweet-scented flowers lead south to Manaccan at the head of a tidal creek. Just east of Helford Passage is the National Trust's delightful Glendurgan Gardens containing rare and exotic plants.

HELSTON
MAP REF: 90SW6527

The 'quaint old Cornish town' of the well-known song is decked with flags and flowers on 8 May for Flora Day, a celebration to welcome spring dating back to the 17th century. No song is sung, and the rather formal, jigging dance is known not as the Floral but the Furry, from the Cornish word *fer* or Feast Day.

Helston was once a thriving port and ships sailed the Loe River to load locally streamed tin, but during the 13th century a bar of shingle formed at the mouth of the river, cutting off access to the sea. The freshwater lake, Loe Pool, that built up behind the barrier is one of the two sites in Cornwall reputed to be where King Arthur's sword, Excalibur, was received by a hand rising from the water. (See also 'Bodmin Moor'.) A

◀ The peaceful setting of Lamorna Cove, with granite quarry in the background

LAMORNA
MAP REF: 90SW4424

Set between headlands of golden granite is Lamorna Cove, as peaceful and beautiful as its name suggests, with a small crescent of sand, a stout stone pier and a sprinkling of cottages. To one side is a granite quarry from where stone was cut to build the Thames Embankment and several lighthouses. A flower-bordered lane leads up a deep sheltered combe to the tiny village and an old flour-mill. The famous inn, The Wink, was originally only licensed to sell beer, but a wink to the landlord would produce something a little stronger. Another suggestion is that the winking worthy on the pub's famous sign was either a local vicar or dignitary closing one eye as the 'gentlemen (smugglers) go by.....' Follow the road up the valley and turn left to reach, after ¾ mile, The Merry Maidens, a Bronze Age circle of 19 stones said to be a group of young girls turned to granite for dancing on the Sabbath. Two large standing stones in nearby fields, The Pipers, are reputed to be the musicians who accompanied the dancers and met the same fate.

LAND'S END
MAP REF: 90SW3425

Known as Belerion, 'Seat of Storms', to the Romans, this most westerly point in mainland England has been under new ownership since 1987 and has been extensively improved. It has long been a major attraction to visitors and now offers a series of first class exhibitions and facilities to complement its spectacular natural attractions. The focus of the 'Land's End Experience' is the 'Last Labyrinth', an audio-visual presentation on the grand scale. There are a number of craft shops. Additional exhibitions outline the wildlife, geology and maritime history of the area while there is an exhibition of some of the finest hand-crafted model sailing ships in the country. The refurbished State House Hotel has breathtaking sea views. There are numerous attractions and facilities for children.

Walk south from the hotel along the coastal footpath to witness some of the most magnificent cliff scenery in Britain. Beyond the jutting reefs of Enys Dodnan and the Armed Knight lies the Longships Lighthouse on its sea-blasted reef. On the horizon are the Wolf Rock lighthouse and the Isles of Scilly, 28 miles distant. South-east, just over a mile away in Nanjizal Bay, archways of orange lichen-encrusted granite rise from a dazzling ultramarine sea.

LANHYDROCK HOUSE
MAP REF: 92SX0863

Lanhydrock belonged to the Augustinian Priory of St Petroc at nearby Bodmin before being surrendered to Henry VIII in 1539. Bought by the Robartes family in 1620, it remained their home until it was given to the National Trust, together with 400 acres of surrounding land, in 1953. Built amidst wooded parkland on the edge of the Fowey valley, the house is approached along an avenue of beech trees. It appears to be Tudor, but the majority of the 17th-century house was destroyed by fire in 1881. The charming entrance porch and north wing remain intact, but the remainder of the house is a Victorian copy in the Tudor style. The interior provides a vivid picture of life in Victorian times, particularly 'below stairs'. Her Ladyship's room, the dining room, steward's room, drawing room and the Long Gallery are all worthy of inspection. On the hillside behind the house is the 15th-century Church of St Hydrock, and the surrounding gardens are a mass of colour in early summer.

◄ The magnificent 17th-century plaster ceiling in Lanhydrock's Long Gallery

LANLIVERY
MAP REF: 92SX0859

The 15th-century tower of Lanlivery church stands almost 100ft high and is one of the finest in Cornwall. Next to the old village inn is Churchtown Field Studies Centre where mentally and physically handicapped youngsters come to enjoy activity holidays. A road and then a footpath running north-west lead to the summit of Helman Tor with its rocking logan stone which lies just below the summit on the south-west side. There are traces of a possible Neolithic settlement (about 3,000BC) on the hilltop. South of the main top is a huge pile of flat boulders called the Cup and Saucer Rock.

LAUNCESTON
MAP REF: 95SX3384

Known as 'Lanson' by the local people, this old market town close to the Devon border is proudly Cornish and has retained much of its character. Built on a hill topped by a Norman castle, the town's origins lie across the valley of the River Kensey to the north where a community grew up around an Augustinian priory and the Church of St Stephen. It is here that you will find the 15th-century mother church of Launceston and the Byzantine-style Roman Catholic church, built early this century. On the south side of a medieval footbridge spanning the Kensey is the tiny Church of St Thomas, built in 1182, which contains the largest font in Cornwall. The castle which dominates the town was built following the Norman Conquest, but the outer and inner baileys are 12th- and 13th-century. Weathering and decay makes the tower of the castle seem a natural part of the great motte or mound on which it is built. Originally called Dunheved, the walled town of narrow streets which grew up around the castle took the name of the neighbouring community and eventually became the capital of Cornwall, only relinquishing that title in 1838 when the Right of Assize passed to Bodmin.

The finest stonemasons in Cornwall were assembled by Sir Henry Trecarrel to decorate St Mary Magdalene Church in memory of his wife. The profusion of carvings reflects the style of the times carried to extremes. The church was built between 1511 and 1524. As well as several well-preserved redbrick Georgian houses, this busy shopping centre also boasts a smart art gallery over the South Gate and a local history museum in Lawrence House. Launceston Leisure Centre at Coronation Park has numerous sport and leisure facilities including an indoor pool. To the west of the town, Launceston Steam Railway runs along the beautiful Kensey valley. The secret world of the wild otter can be experienced at the Tamar Otter Park at North Petherwin, north of Launceston.

▼ The cliffs at Land's End and (inset), the keep of the Norman Launceston Castle

LELANT
MAP REF: 90SW5437

Lelant grew as a flourishing port on the western bank of the Hayle estuary in the Middle Ages, but as the river became clogged with silt, so its importance declined. The estuary marshland, known as the Saltings, is now a sanctuary for wading birds, and cars can be left at the nearby station before a journey along the scenic rail line to St Ives. The village's golf course, renowned in the golfing world, offers fine views across to Hayle Towans and Godrevy lighthouse, and nestling in the dunes at its edge is the 15th-century church dedicated to St Uny, a 6th-century Irish saint and the brother of St Ia who founded St Ives. The church was in constant danger of being engulfed by drifting sand from the great mouth of St Ives Bay. In the 18th century marram grass was planted extensively to stabilise the sand.

The 500-acre tidal estuary of the Lelant Saltings is now an official RSPB Reserve and was transferred to the Society in return for a nominal sum as part of a management plan for the development of the Hayle Harbour area and part of the Lelant shoreline.

LISKEARD
MAP REF: 92SX2564

Today Liskeard is a busy market town of great charm, serving a wide agricultural community, but it was once one of Cornwall's stannary towns (for the testing of tin), and its prosperity was enhanced by the rich copper ore from the nearby Caradon mines and the granite from Cheesewring quarry. Standing at the head of a river valley, Liskeard was linked to the port of Looe by a canal early last century. This was superseded in 1859 by the railway line which now carries visitors down to the coast. Buildings of note include Cornwall's largest parish church, several Georgian houses, a Victorian Italianate guildhall, an 1833 coaching inn and Stuart House where King Charles I stayed in 1644. The waters of the Pipe Well are reputed to have certain therapeutic powers.

To the west of Liskeard is one of Cornwall's foremost tourist attractions, Dobwalls Theme Park with one of the biggest adventure playgrounds in the country. Other attractions include the Forest Railroad and 'Mr Thorburn's Edwardian Countryside', where the wildlife paintings of Archibald Thorburn are displayed in period settings.

▲ Looking towards Liskeard's Fore Street

LIZARD
MAP REF: 91SW7012

Lizard Point is the most southerly point on the British mainland, and it was from these cliffs that the approaching Spanish Armada was first sighted in 1588. The first lighthouse on The Lizard was established in 1620, using open coal fires. It was erected by Sir John Killigrew of the notorious Arwennack family of Falmouth. Shipowners refused to pay fees to support the venture and even accused Killigrew of averting potential wrecks on The Lizard so that they might be wrecked within his own territory further up the coast, where he held rights of salvage. It was not until 1752 that a regular light was established at The Lizard. It was taken over officially by Trinity House in 1790 and converted from coal to oil in 1815. Today's immensely powerful light can be seen at a distance of 64 miles on a clear night.

On the windswept tip of the high peninsula, the village of Lizard is the only British mainland community lying south of the 50th parallel. Almost the entire Lizard Peninsula is composed of soft, colourful serpentine stone, ideal for carving in local workshops. The surrounding heathland is a botanist's paradise and supports many rare plants. East of the village are the pretty hamlet of Landewednack and the Church of St Winwalloe, built of alternate serpentine and granite blocks. Just west of The Lizard is the National Trust's Kynance Cove with its exquisite golden sands and isolated tidal pinnacles of multicoloured serpentine. They have fascinating names like The Bishop, The Bellows and Sugarloaf.

▲ Inset: Looe's fishermen mending their nets within the harbour

▲ Main picture: Looe's bustling and picturesque harbour

LOOE
MAP REF: 92SX2553

Looe is two for the price of one, East and West Looe being separate historical entities joined by an original bridge in 1411. A broad seven-arched bridge now links the two. The town was formerly a pilchard fishing community, and the arrival of the railway in 1859 also brought the first wave of summer visitors to Looe, although tourism's potential was recognised by Looe burgesses as early as 1800, when a 'bathing machine' was established on the beach. The labyrinth of narrow lanes and flower-hung courtyards in the old quarter of East Looe has changed little during the past century, but the remainder of the town is now largely given over to tourism in summer. The bustling quayside is still lined with fishing boats and shark-fishing expeditions can be taken or more leisurely boat trips round St George's Island. Land-based anglers can cast a line from the circular end of the Banjo Pier, or view exotic species of fish in the town's aquarium. The 16th-century guildhall houses a museum display of the town's long history and a nearby former fish cellar now contains a museum of Cornish folk items.

To the south of Looe lies St George's Island, once inhabited in the distant past by the alleged pirate, smuggler and general rascal 'Black Joan' and her brother Fyn.

▼ Inset: the tools of one of Lizard's serpentine stone carvers

▲ Asparagus Island, just off Kynance Cove

LOSTWITHIEL
MAP REF: 92SX1059

One of the most attractive and interesting small market towns in Cornwall, Lostwithiel was its capital for a short period in the 13th century, before passing that honour to Launceston. The town grew to prominence as the lowest bridging point on the River Fowey. It prospered from the profits of tin and wool, becoming the seat of the Duchy Parliament, Stannary Court and Hall of Exchequer.

Between Lostwithiel and Restormel Castle to the north lies the site of what was the biggest iron mine in Cornwall. A tramway took ores to Lostwithiel where they were loaded

▼ Main picture: the impressive ruins of the Norman Restormel Castle, perched on a hilltop site

on to barges and taken to Fowey for shipment. Today Lostwithiel is a peaceful place to browse round antique and craft shops, enjoying the well-preserved Georgian houses, narrow 'ope-ways' and old shopfronts before relaxing in the riverside gardens. A dark, cobbled passageway leads beneath an arch in the buttressed walls of the 13th-century Old Duchy Palace. Dating from the same period is the unusual octagonal Breton-style spire of St Bartholomew's Church. The town's guildhall, built in 1740, houses a small local history museum. North of the town a road between flat meadows and Duchy of Cornwall woodlands leads to Restormel Castle; a remarkably well-preserved and fine example of a Norman castle.

A short drive from Lostwithiel down the eastern bank of the River Fowey leads to the Church of St Winnow, which contains some colourful 15th-century glass.

THE DUCHY OF CORNWALL

The Duchy of Cornwall refers not to the entire county, but only to the estates owned by the Duke of Cornwall; mainly farms, woodlands and a few castles. The title also refers to the many Duchy estates and properties outside Cornwall.

The Duchy was created by

▲ As the eldest son of the monarch Prince Charles is the current Duke of Cornwall

Edward III as an estate for the eldest son of the monarch. In 1337 Edward the Black Prince rode to Launceston castle to be proclaimed the first Duke of Cornwall and to meet his tenants.

HRH Prince Charles became Duke of Cornwall at the age of four, on his mother's accession to the throne. In 1973 he too travelled to Launceston to be proclaimed the 24th Duke and to meet his tenants. He also received his feudal dues, an extraordinary collection of items which included a pair of white gloves, a brace of greyhounds, a pound each of pepper and the herb cummin, a bow de 'arburne, a pair of gilt spurs, 100 specially struck silver shillings, a carriage of wood to be delivered daily and a salmon spear.

The Prince receives nothing from the Civil List, his only income being derived from the Duchy. As chairman of the Prince's Council, he is ultimately responsible for the management of some 128,000 acres of land comprising almost 200 farms, leased to tenant farmers, and 2,400 acres of woodlands, all of which play an important role in Cornwall's economy. The Duke takes a personal interest in the estate's management, making frequent visits to its woodlands, farms, sawmills and nurseries, even occasionally lending a hand with the milking of cows, planting of crops and building of walls.

▲ Votive offerings of rag hang from the trees surrounding Madron Wishing Well

The National Trust gardens of Trengwainton, south of Madron, are rich in semi-tropical plants. The moorland to the north of Madron is rich in prehistoric relics. Two miles along the road to Morvah stands Lanyon Quoit, an exposed Neolithic chamber-tomb consisting of a mighty capstone supported by three upright stones. Just under a mile further on a rough track, signposted, leads to the Mên-an-Tol or 'holed stone' which stands between two upright stones. Local children were said to be cured of rickets by being passed through the stone against the sun. In a field further along the track stands Maen Scryfa or 'inscribed stone', said to mark the grave of a 6th-century chieftain.

LUXULYAN
MAP REF: 92SX0558

The densely-forested Luxulyan Valley winding north from St Blazey is a favourite springtime beauty spot with local people. A mighty viaduct, built by local mine and quarry-owner Joseph Treffry in 1842, carried a mineral line and aqueduct across the valley to the port of Par. The village of Luxulyan contains some interesting cottages which are built from locally-quarried granite, as are the fine 15th-century church and turreted tower. At the lower end of the village is St Cyor's Holy Well, now dried up, beneath a stone canopy. A narrow lane leads north to Lowertown and across the flat, wooded expanse of Breney Common to the high vantage point of Helman Tor.

MADRON
MAP REF: 90SW4531

At Madron the mother church of Penzance dedicated to St Madernus stands on the green heights above the town. A broad wagon roof spans the church, where you can see some old carved bench-ends and the Trafalgar Banner, commemorating the first news of the victory and the death of Nelson in 1805. A mile north of the village a path winds through a thicket of gnarled lichen-encrusted trees to an ancient roofless baptistry with its small, stone altar. Nearby is Madron Wishing Well whose waters are said to possess healing powers. Votive offerings of scraps of rags are still found hanging from the branches of surrounding trees.

MARAZION
MAP REF: 90SW5130

Facing St Michael's Mount, to which it is linked by a cobbled causeway negotiable at low tide, Marazion is a town of great antiquity. The town's delightful name has no connection with 'Zion'. It was once the civic centre and main market of the Mount's Bay area and its name derived from *Marghas Vyghan*, Cornish for 'Little Market', just as Market Jew Street in Penzance stems from *Marghas Yow* or 'Thursday Market'.

The fine expanse of beach running west from Marazion has become noted for good windsurfing and a number of international championship contests are held here. Just across the road from the beaches is Marazion Marsh traversed by the Penzance-Paddington railway line,

◄ The Mên-an-Tol stone near Lanyon, a holed stone between two upright ones whose regular trains in no way affect the many nesting and roosting birds within the pools and reed beds. Throughout the early part of the year millions of starlings roost in the marshes. Their incoming flight at dusk is a roadside spectacular.

MAWGAN
MAP REF: 91SW7125

This string of pretty cottages, inn, shop and church lies in a wooded valley south of the Helford River. To the north are deep, winding creeks and to the south, the flat, exposed heathland of the Lizard plateau. Trelowarren, for 500 years the home of the Vyvyan family, lies in parkland nearby. This Tudor house has a neo-Gothic chapel and the stables to the rear contain a restaurant and craft centre.

The Lizard Downs to the south are dominated by the huge communication dishes of British Telecom's Satellite Earth Station at Goonhilly. The station is open to the public and there is a visitor centre where modern technology sits side-by-side with items from the surrounding Neolithic burial sites of 5,000 years ago.

MAWNAN SMITH
MAP REF: 91SW7827

Exotic and semi-tropical plants flourish in the mild coastal area surrounding this quiet village with its thatched inn and cottages. The 13th-century church stands amidst trees on the cliff-edge overlooking the mouth of the Helford River. To the north of the village are the gardens of Penjerrick where lawns and fine shrubs surround a house belonging to the Fox family. To the east is Rosemullion Head, which is strewn with colourful wild flowers in spring and summer. Along the riverbank to the west is Helford Passage with its waterside Ferry Boat Inn and passenger ferry across to Helford on the opposite bank. Tortuous lanes lead west from Mawnan Smith to Porth Navas, a creekside hamlet popular with the yachting fraternity and famed for its oysters; grown in beds owned by the Duchy of Cornwall Oyster Farm.

▼ The lush riverside gardens of Glendurgan, south of Mawnan Smith

SMUGGLERS AND WRECKERS

▲ Jamaica Inn, once a smugglers' refuge

The nefarious pursuit of smuggling, once described as a 'national failing', was nowhere more common than in Cornwall. Remote from the rest of England and easily accessible from the Continent, it was here that the practice reached its height during the 18th century. Wine, spirits, tobacco and bullion were the principal items brought ashore by the 'free-traders'. All levels of society were involved in this stealthy evasion of the revenue laws.

Most notable of the Cornish smugglers were John and Harry Carter who operated in Mount's Bay, three miles up the coast from Marazion. As a boy John Carter called himself 'The King of Prussia' after his hero Frederick the Great. The name stuck, and one of the deep inlets from which he operated became known as Prussia Cove. Devout Methodists (swearing was forbidden in their company), the brothers owned a 160-ton cutter with 19 guns which they used for smuggling runs to Brittany. The Carters mounted a battery of small cannon on the clifftop near their base, and on one occasion, when the revenue cutter *Faery* chased a smuggling boat into the cove, the brothers opened fire, and kept up the cannonade until the cutter withdrew. The inns, cottages, manor houses and, occasionally, churches of outlying fishing communities had secret caches in their walls or under their floors for concealing contraband.

Wrecking, the practice of looting wrecked ships, was also a regular and often necessary way of life in Cornwall, for wages were low and poverty rife. In its mildest form it amounted to little more than beachcombing; gleaning from the shore what the sea had thrown up and still practiced today in search of timber and fishing floats. Less often it consisted of the organised plundering of the vessel itself, sometimes with scant regard for the well-being of any crew still aboard. Tales of wreckers cold-bloodedly drowning sailors while they fought for cargo were not uncommon, but stories of wreckers deliberately luring ships on to the rocky coast at night by means of false lights contain little, if any, truth. The attitude of most Cornish wreckers was best expressed by Parson Troutbeck of Scilly: 'We pray, O Lord, not that wrecks should occur, but that if they do, Thou wilt drive them into the Scilly Isles, for the benefit of the poor inhabitants.'

SS Brest, wrecked at Lizard Point, 1879 ▶

MEVAGISSEY

MAP REF: 92SX0144

This famous and lovely fishing village acquired its name in the late 15th century from the Welsh and Irish Saints, Meva and Itha. It was previously known as Porthilly. Rows of colour-washed cob cottages descend the steep sides of a valley to a picturesque natural harbour bobbing with boats.

Mevagissey is still a flourishing fishing port although tourists have tended to replace pilchards as a source of income in recent years. Early this century over 100 luggers crammed into the inner harbour which was lined with fishing-stores and net-lofts. The handsome quayside building known as 'The Shark's Fin' reflects the port's industrious past. Pilchards were salted in deep quayside pits before being pressed into barrels by the fishwives. Pack-mules carried baskets of fish through the streets, though some were so narrow that the baskets had to be carried on poles by men, one behind the other. As well as providing tasty food, pilchards also provided oil which was used in lamps for light and warmth, hence the local fishermen's rhyme: 'Food, heat and light, All in one night.'

Despite the proliferation of gift shops and cafés, the old port has retained much of its character and its leaning buildings and quaint courtyards are hung with flowers in summertime.

Mevagissey was noted for building very fast sailing luggers and the tradition of fine boat-building is maintained at Portmellon, just south of Mevagissey, where numerous famous Cornish fishing boats have been built as well as fine yachts. Further south still is the charming village of Gorran Haven which sustained a strong fishing rivalry with Mevagissey in the great days of the pilchard. One of Cornwall's most famous headlands, the formidable Dodman Point, lies south-east of Gorran.

MINIONS

MAP REF: 95SX2671

This exposed and sturdy village stands on the south-eastern edge of Bodmin Moor amidst a compelling landscape of bare moorland, old quarries and ancient stones. It boasts the highest pub in Cornwall, a popular place with the quarry workers and miners who lived here up to this century. Blue-grey granite from nearby Cheesewring quarry and rich copper, tin and lead ore from the Caradon mines were transported by rail from here to Looe. On the rim of the quarry stands the Cheesewring itself, a strange natural formation of flattish rocks. Below and to the left of the quarry are the remnants of a cave used as a dwelling by the gifted 18th-century stone-cutter and thinker, Daniel Gumb. Gumb's large family lived in what was originally a much larger cave enclosure with several rooms. He was self-taught in astronomy and geometry. The surviving roof has one of Euclid's problems carved upon it.

Just west of Minions are The Hurlers, three Bronze Age stone circles said to be men turned to stone for playing the Cornish sport of hurling on a Sunday.

MORWENSTOW

MAP REF: 95SS2015

The great cliffs of the Morwenstow coast are the highest and wildest in Cornwall yet the surrounding countryside is delightfully pastoral and peaceful. The hamlet of Morwenstow is best known for its eccentric vicar-cum-poet, Robert Stephen Hawker. He came to this thinly populated parish in 1834 and spent 40 years serving 'a mixed multitude of smugglers, wreckers and dissenters'.

Hawker was much concerned with the fate of mariners wrecked on this treacherous coast and often scrambled down the high cliffs to carry back the bodies of drowned seamen for a Christian burial. He strode around the parish in long sea-boots, a fisherman's jersey and a purple coat and spent much time

FISHING

With over 250 miles of coastline, it is hardly surprising that fishing has been practised in Cornwall since Neolithic times. The heyday of the industry was between the mid-18th and mid-19th centuries, when every harbour, cove and inlet had its own fishing fleet. They served the local need for cheap food and provided France, Italy and Spain with a necessary requirement for Lent and fast days. Pilchards were the basis of the industry. They arrived in huge shoals close to the shore and were trapped by seine nets strung between three or four boats. A 'huer' posted on a nearby cliff would direct operations by signalling with a trumpet or white hoops. His semaphore-like signals and cry of 'Hevva!' gave the exact position of the shoal, allowing the boats to manoeuvre the net accurately, ready for 'shooting'.

Pilchard catches were enormous, and it is recorded that in 1834, at St Ives, 10,000 hogshead of pilchard (30 million fish) were landed in just one hour. Most harbours had at least one fish cellar or 'palace', a large

▼ The old town near the harbour at Mevagissey

◀ The Cheeswring, a natural rock formation near Minions

MAP REF: 90SW4626

This lovliest of Cornish fishing villages still retains its structural charm and identity although there is little full-time fishing. A hundred years ago it was possible to traverse Mousehole Harbour dry-shod by walking across the decks of pilchard boats. The crucial pronunciation of the village's enchanting name is 'Mouzel'. The source of the name is obscure but is certainly old Cornish.

The whole form and shape of Mousehole is perfectly Cornish. Narrow lanes and passageways flanked by traditional granite cottages encircle a fine little harbour of striking granite block construction. Offshore is St Clement's Isle, site of an ancient chapel.

In 1595 the village was raided by Spanish privateers and razed to the ground. The only building to survive was the manor house, later to become the Keigwin Arms Inn and now a private dwelling. A modern tragedy devastated Mousehole on the dark night of 19 December 1981

writing poetry and smoking opium in a cliff-edge hut made of driftwood. The hut is now in the care of the National Trust, as is a large area surrounding Morwenstow except for the church and its environs. Best remembered for reviving the custom of the Harvest Festival and for his poem, *The Song of the Western Men*, which has become the Cornish national anthem, Hawker is also renowned for dressing up as a mermaid and for excommunicating one of his cats for catching a mouse on Sunday.

The doorway of the part-Norman church is carved with the heads of men and beasts, and the unusual chimneys of the adjacent rectory are based on two Oxford colleges, three church towers and Hawker's mother's gravestone.

▲ Picturesque Mousehole harbour

undercover courtyard where the fish were salted, packed into barrels and pressed before being shipped overseas. The fish oil by-product was used as lamp fuel and rotten fish were spread on the fields as fertiliser. The decline of the pilchard shoals has been attributed to massive overfishing, but climatic changes leading to changes in water temperature and the unquantifiable behaviour of pelagic fish are possible factors. The Cornish fishing industry diversified throughout the first half of this century. Through necessity, hard work and skill the Cornish fisherman became one of the most versatile of all.

The modern industry in Cornwall has seen a typical boom and slump pattern. It has survived intact although increasingly under threat from 'paper fish' regulations as the EC strives to regulate a diminishing and difficult resource. Newlyn in the far west has grossed the biggest landings in England for several years and is a major UK fish market. Its fleet of nearly 200 vessels pursue all types of fishing including crab and lobster potting; hand-lining for mackerel; traditional trawling and

beam-trawling for mixed fish like dover sole, plaice, ray, cod and whiting. During the past decade, extensive gill-netting for ling, pollack, hake and dogfish has produced an enterprising fleet of far-ranging vessels. Other Cornish ports like Looe, Polperro, Mevagissey, Falmouth, and Newquay have smaller but no less viable fleets while dozens of famous coves and small harbours still sustain some kind of fishery. The future is difficult but the powerful traditions and expertise of the Cornish fishermen still survive and give the county much of its unique value.

▼ Fishing boats returning to Newlyn

when the eight-man crew of the local lifeboat the *Solomon Browne* was lost during a savage south-easterly gale gusting to hurricane force 12. The lifeboat had rescued four of the crew of the coaster *Union Star* which had been driven relentlessly on to the grinding cliffs west of Lamorna. In an act of unsurpassed courage the lifeboatmen made a final rescue bid in mountainous seas for the remaining four crewmen on the coaster. Tragically, lifeboat and coaster were lost with all hands.

Tom Bawcock's Eve, celebrated every 23 December, recalls the time a local fisherman saved the village from famine by sailing out in a storm and returning with a large catch of seven sorts of fish. A special dish, starry-gazy pie, with fish-heads poking up through the pastry, is still baked and eaten in his honour.

Injured and oiled birds are cared for at Mousehole Bird Sanctuary. At Paul, one mile inland, the prominent church tower acts as a day-mark to shipping. In the churchyard is a memorial to Dolly Pentreath, the fishwife who died in 1777 and is said to have been the last person to converse only in Cornish. There has been a healthy revival of the language in recent years.

MULLION
MAP REF: 91SW6719

This compactly grouped village of sturdy cottages has at its centre a broad-towered church inside which are some remarkable carved bench-ends depicting surprisingly bawdy scenes. A road descends 200ft from the edge of the Lizard plateau to Mullion harbour, whose solid granite piers were built in the 1890s. The harbour is owned by the National Trust. A charming old net store, a winch house and wooden fish cellar survive. Exhilarating footpath walks lead north to Polurrian beach or south over cliffs of scented thyme and sea-thrift to Kynance Cove.

THE MYLORS
MAP REF: 91SW8235

The wooded surroundings of Mylor Village and Mylor Peninsula are in rich contrast to the more open coastal cliff areas of Cornwall. The village is easily reached from Falmouth-Penryn. It stands at the head of Mylor Creek, one of the many arms of Carrick Roads the famous deep water anchorage of Falmouth. Mylor had close connections with the packet sailing ships which delivered mail world-wide until the advent of steamships last century. Many of the old packet skippers are buried in the churchyard of the exquisitely placed St Melanus Church, which also boasts some amusing tombstone inscriptions including that of Joseph Crapp, a local shipwright, who died in 1770. It reads:

Alass frend Joseph
His end was all most Sudden
As thou a mandate came
Express from Heaven –
His foot, it slip and he did fall
Help help he cries, and that was all.

Restronguet Weir and Restronguet Passage with their creekside charm on the eastern edge of the Peninsula, can be reached easily from Mylor Village.

NEWLYN
MAP REF: 90SW4628

Newlyn is the major fishing port of the south-west and has been a leader in England's fishing industry over recent years for total value of fish landed. It is an ancient port with a vigorous tradition and is an international 'harbour of refuge'. The town climbs steeply from the great open mouth of the harbour and there is a refreshing and invigorating early morning atmosphere of bustle and enterprise round Newlyn's recently extended and refurbished fish market. Architecturally Newlyn still retains

some of its traditional cottages and houses linked by alleyways and courts. However, 135 properties were demolished with their traditional infrastructure in 1937 in a bout of local government excess. This was in spite of a remarkable campaign against the scheme which culminated in an historic voyage from Newlyn to the quay of the Houses of Parliament by the Newlyn fishing lugger *Rosebud*. It was a spectacular piece of lobbying for the time and although the crew, in their 'working best', were greeted with cream teas and sympathy by a government minister, they lost the day.

The greatly extended piers at Newlyn enclose a small 15th-century harbour, but the port is emphatically 20th-century in terms of its modern fleet of over 200 vessels ranging from small 20ft boats through a large

◀ One of the solid granite piers of Mullion's 19th-century harbour

middle-size fleet of 30–60ft vessels and up to 100ft beam trawlers. The huge volume of fish landed at Newlyn is shipped to Billingsgate and all over Europe by massive freezer lorries and the port has a reputation for the high quality of its products.

The town also has a great artistic tradition dating from the founding during the late 18th century of what became known as the Newlyn School of Painting, part of an international movement based on the *plein-air* style of painting with its emphasis on outdoor subjects. It was the clear light and bustling life of the port that attracted the artist Stanhope Forbes, founder of the Newlyn School of Artists. Its best-known members were Frank Bramley, Norman Garstin, Lamorna Birch, Alfred Munnings and Laura Knight, and examples of their work, together with paintings and sculpture by the present-day generation of Newlyn artists, can be seen in Newlyn-Orion Art Gallery and at Penlee House in Penzance.

NEWQUAY
MAP REF: 91SW8161

Newquay was originally a tiny fishing village called Towan Blistra, a colourful name supplanted by the prosaic New Quay when a pier was added in the 15th century. Pilchard fishing was inevitably a major business until the end of last century when Victorian visitors became attracted to Newquay's bracing

beaches. Large hotels soon sprang up in the town and on the grassy headlands. The arrival of the railway greatly expanded the tourism potential. Now Cornwall's largest and most popular holiday resort, with all the attendant facilities, Newquay overlooks several fine sandy beaches sheltered by spectacular high cliffs and headlands. Surfers can enjoy the high, green Atlantic rollers of Fistral beach; young couples the lively nightlife; and families the wide range of indoor and outdoor entertainment. There is an excellent golf course, a boating lake and a large zoo in Trenance Park. Newquay is a surfers' Mecca and venue for championship contests.

Not far from the town are other major attractions like the Lappa Valley Railway at St Newlyn East, Dairyland and the Country Life Museum at Summercourt. In a peaceful, wooded valley a few miles south-east from bustling Newquay is the gabled Elizabethan manor house of Trerice, owned by the National Trust. Rebuilt in 1571 by Sir John Arundell, it contains fine moulded plaster ceilings, broad fireplaces, walnut and oak furniture and several colourful tapestries. The hall, overlooked by a musician's gallery, is lit by a vast window containing 576 panes of glass. The house is surrounded by well-tended gardens and in the grounds a barn contains an unusual Museum of Lawnmowers.

Newquay is a popular resort ▶

▲ Newlyn is still an artists' Mecca

▼ Dawn rising over Newlyn's large fleet, moored up in the harbour

THE ART COLONIES

The mild climate, the exceptionally clear light and Mediterranean atmosphere which first attracted artists to west Cornwall over a century ago still draw them today, and the area west of Hayle probably contains the greatest concentration of painters, sculptors and craftsmen anywhere in Britain outside London.

In the 19th century, as today, the artistic life of Cornwall centred around the fishing villages of St Ives and Newlyn, 10 miles apart on opposite sides of the Penwith peninsula. The Irish painter Stanhope Forbes arrived in Newlyn for a few days in 1884, and stayed on. He met several other painters whom he had known in Brittany and, together with Walter Langley, Frank Bramley, Norman Garstin and Elizabeth Armstrong (later to become his wife), Forbes formed the Newlyn School of Painting. The rocky coastline, sheltered valleys, high moorland and granite outcrops provided ideal subject-matter for their paintings, but their most famous works portrayed the day-to-day life of the fishing village itself. The same period also found many largely foreign artists settling in St Ives. Anders Zorn, Louis Grier, Julius Olsson, Algernon Talmage, Adrian Stokes, Borlase Smart and Arnesby Brown all set up studios, and formed the St Ives Arts Club in 1888.

The early years of this century found a revival of spirit in Newlyn with the arrival of Laura Knight and Dod Procter. Together with S J Lamorna Birch they produced many fine landscape paintings of the coast south of Newlyn. The 1920s found the leading artists Ben Nicholson and Christopher Wood settling in St Ives where they 'discovered' Alfred Wallis, a retired fisherman whose primitive paintings on scraps of wood were to prove very influential.

Nicholson's first wife, the sculptor Barbara Hepworth, began to work in the town and the world-famous potter Bernard Leach set up the Leach Pottery at Higher Stennack. By the 1960s a new generation of artists had joined the St Ives colony, including Roger Hilton, Peter Lanyon, Bryan Wynter, Terry Frost and Patrick Heron. As St Ives has developed as a tourist

▲ A painting by one of the Newlyn School

town so many artists have moved to nearby villages, and examples of work by the leading artists can be seen in the Penwith Society of Arts gallery in Back Road West, and the St Ives Society of Artists gallery in the old Mariners' Church in Norway Square. The Wills Lane Gallery and the Salt House Gallery also contain recent work by the latest generation of St Ives artists. Many sculptures by Dame Barbara Hepworth, together with her workshop and tools, can be seen at the Barbara Hepworth Museum in Back Street. St Ives' position as an arts Mecca seems even more assured with the scheduled completion in 1992 of a specially built St Ives Gallery to house the Tate Gallery's collection of paintings of the St Ives School.

A permanent exhibition of paintings by members of the Newlyn School is on show at Penlee House in Penzance's Morrab Gardens, while the distinguished and innovative Newlyn-Orion Gallery continues to maintain a vigorous programme of exhibitions by leading artists.

PADSTOW
MAP REF: 92SW9175

Its sheltered position in the Camel estuary makes Padstow a welcome north-coast haven for shipping. It became an important trading and shipbuilding port, but the formation of the Doom Bar sandbank across the mouth of the estuary prevented large vessels using the harbour. Nevertheless, before World War II it was an important fishing port. It declined after the war but now has a good fleet of vessels.

The attractive medieval town has remained largely unspoilt. Abbey House on the South Quay dates from the 15th century while the Court House of Sir Walter Raleigh stands on the North Quay. Many emigrants left for America last century from the harbour. St Petroc, Cornwall's chief saint, landed at Padstow from Ireland

Boats at anchor in Penzance' sheltered harbour, whose long piers were built as protection against pirates ▶

PAR
MAP REF: 92SX0753

The industrialist Joseph Treffry built the port of Par on reclaimed land. The port was used for many years as an outlet for china clay from the St Austell clay country and its industrialisation is complete although now in decline. Par was noted for its shipbuilding, and schooners for the Newfoundland trade were built here.

South-west of the town, at Biscovey, are the Mid-Cornwall Galleries and Craft Centre. Before the building of the port, the sea reached as far inland as the village of Tywardreath, or 'House on the strand', a charming group of buildings immortalised in a

and the sea is one of the richest areas of industrial archaeology in Britain. Mine stacks and engine houses and the scattered remains of mine treatment works cover the coast for nearly two miles. There is a Visitor

▲ The accordian band leads a way through the streets of Padstow on May Day

in the 6th century, and the church dedicated to him has a fine Elizabethan pulpit and some amusing bench-ends. Prideaux Place stands at the top of the town and is open to the public at certain times.

One of the great Padstow traditions is the May Day celebration of the Hobby Horse, a rumbustious and lively affair with strong undertones of pagan fertility rites merged with legend and historical event. The 'Obby Oss' is a dramatic concoction of ferocious mask, flowing plume, black hooped gown and fierce wooden 'snappers'. It is carried and manipulated from within by a member of the Obby Oss 'gang' and preceded by a 'teaser' with a club in a tireless and wild dance to the excellent 'May Morning Song'.

Daphne du Maurier novel of that name. At Polmear, east of Par, stands a delightful row of old almshouses. From here a road leads south to the tiny sandy cove of Polkerris with its small pier and Elizabethan pilchard cellar. A cliff-top walk south leads to the red-and-white striped beacon on Gribbin Head.

PENDEEN
MAP REF: 90SW3834

The Pendeen area is the heartland of Cornwall's coastal mining country. It is part of a mile-long straggle of small communities comprising Carnyorth, Trewellard, Boscaswell and Bojewyan, each one linked to famous coastal mines of last century. The last working mine in the area was at Geevor which finally closed in 1991.

The coastal strip between Pendeen

Centre and mining museum at Geevor.

St John's Church at Pendeen is in the design of the famous cathedral on Iona. It was built by Pendeen miners in the 1850s under the direction of the vicar Robert Aitken who came to the bleak coastal parish in 1849. The stone for the present church came from a quarry on Carn Eanes, the hill above Pendeen. The impressive Pendeen Lighthouse stands on a rocky headland about a mile to the north and is easily reached by road.

PENRYN
MAP REF: 91SW7834

Penryn flourished as a medieval port largely because of Glasney College, a collegiate church and centre of learning founded in the 13th century. It was closed at the Dissolution of the Monasteries, and all that remains is a small fragment of church pillar. The old town with buildings of Tudor, Jacobean and Georgian origins, is designated as a conservation area and has been imaginatively restored.

Penryn was the head of navigation for the Penryn River and was the controlling commercial port throughout the medieval period over what is now Falmouth Harbour. Stone quarried in the nearby parish of Mabe was exported from here last century, but as Falmouth's importance as a port increased, so Penryn's role declined.

Near the village of Mabe Burnthouse, west of Penryn, are Argal and College reservoirs where, with the proper licence, anglers may fish for brown and rainbow trout. The much larger Stithians reservoir, further west, also offers sailing and windsurfing facilities.

PENZANCE

MAP REF: 90SW4730

A lively, spacious town of great character, Penzance is worthy of lengthy exploration. The town's faintly continental name fits its Mediterranean image, but the name seems likeliest to come from the Cornish *pen sans* meaning holy headland. The long arms of the piers were constructed in the 17th century to protect the town from pirates, but not before it had been sacked and partly destroyed, like neighbouring Newlyn and Mousehole, by the Spanish in 1595. It became the chief coinage town for the west of England and its market attracted buyers and sellers from a wide area.

The arrival of the railway in 1859 provided an efficient means of

▼ An attractive street in the centre of Penzance

dispatching locally caught fish, flowers and vegetables direct to London. Its sheltered position at the western end of Mount's Bay and its mild climate also made Penzance a fashionable watering place. Large hotels sprang up and handsome Georgian, Victorian and Regency buildings, terraces and squares can still be found on the south side of the town. The wide main thoroughfare, Market Jew Street, rises in a gentle curve, a high stone-stepped pavement to one side. The name is more prosaic than it sounds and comes from the Cornish *Marghas Yow* meaning Thursday Market. At its head a statue to Penzance's most famous son, Sir Humphry Davy, miners' lamp in hand, stands in front of the Ionic pillars and dome of the Market Hall. Causewayhead, now traffic-free, leads up to a small market and at St John's Hall in Alverton Street is a Geological Museum of great interest.

Chapel Street, the town's most fascinating thoroughfare, is lined with 18th- and 19th-century houses and shopfronts. The elaborate façade of the Georgian Egyptian House faces the Union Hotel, whose Georgian façade hides an Elizabethan interior. Nelson's victory and death were first announced from a minstrel's gallery in the hotel's Assembly Room. At the rear of the building stands the shell of one of the oldest theatres in Britain, which opened in 1787. Further along Chapel Street are the ancient Turk's Head Inn and the Admiral Benbow Inn. Opposite is the Maritime Museum which contains items recovered from wrecks around the coast of Cornwall and the Isles of Scilly. Elizabeth Branwell, mother of

the Brontë sisters, lived in Chapel Street.

Semi-tropical shrubs and flowers surround a Victorian bandstand in Morrab Gardens, while rare trees and shrubs can be seen in Penlee Memorial Gardens, together with a local history museum and paintings by the Newlyn School of Painters in Penlee House. Regular boat and helicopter links with the Isles of Scilly are maintained throughout the year from the harbour where there is also a fascinating National Lighthouse Centre.

Penzance is the ideal starting point for exploring the Land's End Peninsula.

▲ Eroded rocks stand like sculpture on the beach at Perranporth

PERRANPORTH

MAP REF: 91SW7554

This popular family resort lies at the southern end of a three-mile beach of golden sand. Perranporth was originally a mining community but the remains of mine buildings have long ago been swallowed by the encroaching sand. The author Winston Graham wrote the first of his *Poldark* novels here, using a combination of real and fictitious people and places to weave a story of 18th- and 19th-century mining families. To experience the atmosphere of these popular books, walk south along the cliffs to Trevellas Combe and St Agnes.

The odd name of the parish, Perranzabuloe, means 'Piran in the sands', and it was in the centre of the dunes north of Perranporth that the patron saint of tinners, St Piran, founded a chapel in the 6th century.

East of Perranporth, near the village of Rose, is Piran Round, an Iron Age fort transformed into a circular 'playing place', where medieval miracle plays were performed.

▲ The well-protected inner harbour at Polperro whose entrance can be sealed if gales threaten

The Shell House in Polperro's Warren Street is fantastically decorated ▶

POLPERRO
MAP REF: 92SX2051

The most timeless, picturesque and photogenic of all Cornish fishing villages, Polperro nestles in a green valley snaking inland from a small harbour guarded by jagged rocks. Colour-washed cottages rise in tiers above a jumble of unique and intriguing buildings, wound about with narrow alleys. Tales of local smuggling activities concerning rum and tobacco are legion, and it was not by chance that the first Preventive Service station was built nearby. Until the last century, fishing was the chief occupation of the villagers, the smell of pilchards becoming so strong that neighbouring people referred to Polperro as Polstink. Colourful fishing boats still crowd the harbour and the village has retained the atmosphere of a fishing community, with its own fishermen's choir, founded in 1923. Among the many old inns, cottages, studios and gift shops, look for the House-on-Props by the Roman Bridge that leads on to the delightful Warran, a narrow yet sunny alleyway running above the harbour and on to the open cliffs. Parking is restricted to a large car park at the entrance to the village near the historic Crumplehorn Mill.

The National Trust owns most of the coastline to the east and west of Polperro. To the west is a positive switchback of a coastal path. To the east lies Talland Bay and the hamlet of Talland with its fine 13th-century church.

POLZEATH
MAP REF: 94SW9378

The much-loved former poet laureate, Sir John Betjeman, spent many of his childhood holidays on this eastern tip of the Camel estuary, and its villages and church form the subject-matter of many of his poems. From the heights of Rumps Point and Pentire Point to the tamarisk-bordered lanes around Trebetherick, the air is bracing and wild flowers are plentiful.

In 1936 Pentire Head was put on the market and divided into building plots. Yet local protestors roused national concern and enough money was raised to buy the land and present it to the National Trust. High surf breaks on the beach at Polzeath and the cliff caves and rock pools to the south are a children's paradise. The high grassy mound of Brea Hill, south of Trebetherick, looks out over the Doom Bar, a submerged sandbank on which many ships have come to grief. Sheltering behind the hill, on the edge of a golf course, is the tiny Church of St Enodoc, with Betjeman's grave. The church has been almost overwhelmed by the sand several times, and on one occasion, the vicar and congregation had to enter through a hole in the roof. A passenger ferry runs from the nearby village of Rock across the estuary to Padstow.

PORTHCURNO
MAP REF: 90SW3822

A broad beach of white sand dips into a sapphire sea in this small cove, sheltered within the magnificent Porthcurno Bay with its flanking walls of golden granite. Set on the cliffside overlooking the beach is the Minack Open-Air Theatre, a Greek-style amphitheatre where professional theatre companies perform during the summer months. Begun in 1923, it was created by Miss Rowena Cade and offers audiences a spectacular natural backdrop of sea, sand and cliff scenery.

The eastern arm of Porthcurno Bay is made up of the spectacular Treryn

Dinas, a splendid example of an Iron Age cliff castle with its landward earthworks still in place. On the great seaward pinnacles is the famous Logan Rock, a 65-ton monster, once capable of being rocked by hand. Local guides took early 19th-century visitors to view the stone until it was tumbled from its perch by a gang of sailors under Lieutenant Hugh Goldsmith, nephew of the poet Oliver Goldsmith. Local outrage led the Admiralty to instruct Goldsmith to replace the rock, which he did by a remarkable feat of engineering. However, the fine balance of the rocking stone was lost.

Treryn Dinas and the Logan Rock are best reached from the lovely hillside hamlet of Treen ³/₄ mile north-east of Porthcurno.

PORTHLEVEN
MAP REF: 90SW6225

Still a working port with a small fishing fleet and boat-building yard, Porthleven was developed early last century for the export of tin ore. Its long curved harbour is in three sections, the inner one capable of being sealed off from fierce south-westerly gales. This substantial inner basin was a legacy of Victorian enterprise. It was built in the 1850s when there were grandiose plans for the port which never materialised.

Porthleven has a fine open aspect around its harbour area. A terrace of trim Victorian villas lines the east side of the harbour, facing an old waterside inn and lime-kilns, now converted into art galleries. A straggle of old cottages runs east along the crumbling cliff-top above a long, steeply shelving beach. Further along the coast is the shingle barrier of Loe Bar, behind which lies Loe Pool, Cornwall's largest natural lake.

PORT ISAAC
MAP REF: 94SW9980

A fishing harbour since the Middle Ages, this unspoilt huddle of slate cottages and fish cellars is protected by high headlands. The small shingle beach faces an old inn, and narrow alleyways known as 'drangs' wind between the houses. The narrowest is

▲ The long harbour at Portreath

PORTREATH
MAP REF: 90SW6545

Now a popular family beach and small resort, well protected by surrounding high cliffs, Portreath was developed by Francis Basset to serve local mines. The Basset family, who lived at nearby Tehidy estate, owned many of the tin and copper mines in the Redruth area. A long harbour was built for shipping ore and importing Welsh coal to fuel the mine engines.

In 1809 the first railway in Cornwall, and one of the earliest in Britain, was built to link the port with the St Day mining area five miles inland. The remains of the final steep incline section of the railway, used to lower the wagons to Portreath Harbour, can still be seen. Modern houses now stand where huge bins of ore, coal and lime once dominated this remarkable harbour with its hazardous and challenging entrance. To one side of the harbour-mouth stands a white building known as the 'pepper-pot', from where ships were guided into the harbour entrance.

PROBUS
MAP REF: 91SW8947

The tallest church tower in Cornwall – 123ft of magnificently carved moorstone – dominates Probus, once an important wool town. The broad main street leading up to the church boasts some large Georgian houses and old granite cottages with railed steps.

A mile to the east is Trewithen, the 17th-century home of the Hawkins family. Its attractive gardens of rare shrubs, and colourful flowers are open daily, except Sundays, during the summer. Nearby, and also on the A390, is the County Demonstration Garden and Rural Studies Centre where you can compare different varieties of plants, fruit, vegetables and flowers grown under different conditions.

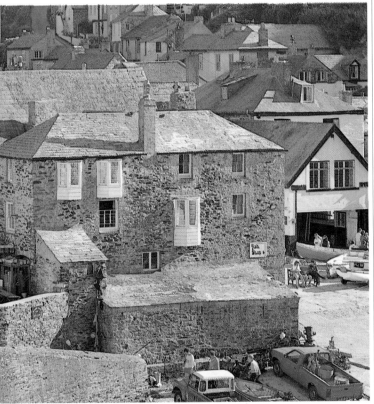

▲ The pretty, unspoilt fishing community of Port Isaac

▼ The Minack Theatre, Porthcurno

known as 'Squeeze-Belly Alley'. There is an inshore lifeboat stationed at Port Isaac. It is housed rather fittingly in the old fish cellars at the head of the harbour. Over the headland to the east is Portgaverne, formerly the main outlet for shipping slate from Delabole which arrived along the 'Great Slate Road'.

West of Port Isaac, and reached by a lane which loops inland, is Portquin, a tiny hamlet at the head of a sheltered inlet, now owned by the National Trust. Overlooking the inlet from a green cliff-top is Doyden Castle, a folly built in 1839. The church at St Kew, a few miles inland, stands in an idyllic streamside setting and has some of the finest medieval glass in Cornwall.

REDRUTH
MAP REF: 91SW6941

Once the capital of Cornish mining, Redruth is an old market town of great character; its architecture ranging in style from Georgian and Gothic to Victorian Italianate and Art Deco. Sprawling on either side of a deep valley, the town contains many interesting nooks and crannies. Its name stems from the Cornish words for the 'red river' which now runs under the foot of the steep main street. In narrow Cross Street is the former home of the Scottish inventor William Murdock. Redruth was the ideal base for such a prolific inventor. Murdock developed lighting from coal-gas and in 1792 his Redruth house was the first in the world to be so lit. He also invented a cast-iron cement, a substitute for isinglass and the vacuum tube carriers used in shops until as late as the 1960s. Murdock also seemed to have patented longevity; dying happily at Redruth aged 86, which for the early 19th century was remarkable.

From the giant spans of the granite railway viaduct at the lower part of the town, a walk up tree-lined Trewirgie Road leads to Redruth's old churchtown. Alongside some well-restored cottages stands the Georgian Church of St Euny, which has a 15th-century tower. The lych-gate covers an extra long coffin-rest for use following major mining accidents.

Towering above Redruth is the bracken-covered hill of Carn Brea,

topped by a memorial to local mine-owner Francis Basset and a dramatically-sited castle. The northern slopes were once thickly wooded and the castle was used in Elizabethan and later times as a hunting lodge. It has been tastefully converted into a restaurant. Neolithic stone ramparts, partly rebuilt in the Iron Age, encircle the twin summits of Carn Brea, which can be reached

▼ A medieval castle built on the 738ft summit of Carn Brea

▲ The Stippy-Stappy of St Agnes

by road from Carnkie. The entire hill is a treasure-house of history and industrial archaeology and is now under the care of the local district authority.

ST AGNES
MAP REF: 91SW7250

This former tin-mining village stands at the head of a steep valley winding down to Trevaunance Cove. The chimneys of ivy-clad engine-houses mark the sites of surrounding mines, bearing such names as Wheal Kitty, Blue Hills and Wheal Friendly. In the centre of the village, a stepped terrace of miners' cottages, known as 'Stippy-Stappy' descends a hill alongside the charming spired church. Lanes lined with old cob cottages and pretty gardens wind off the main street. This bustling village also boasts a handsome Methodist church, several craft workshops and some welcoming pubs. Readers of Winston Graham's *Poldark* novels may recognise St Agnes as the model for the village of St Ann in the books. There is a good small museum of local history, open in the season.

Just outside the village is St Agnes Leisure Park with plentiful attractions set in colourful, landscaped gardens. The Cornish artist John Opie was born in 1761 in a thatched cottage, 'Harmony Cot', east of St Agnes. Examples of his work can be seen in the County Museum in Truro.

Trevaunance Cove, at the mouth of the long combe snaking down from the village, has a popular sand and

shingle beach. Tin ore was shipped from a small 18th-century quay, but this was swept away by a storm in 1934. There were four previous harbours built at St Agnes, starting from 1632. All were swept away.

A footpath along the high cliffs to the west leads to St Agnes Head, with its dramatic view south along the rugged coastline. A walk to the summit of St Agnes Beacon will be rewarded with views as far as the tors of Bodmin Moor. Further south is the charming green valley and cove of Chapel Porth, owned by the National Trust. On the cliff-edge to the north are the mine buildings of Wheal Coates and the Towanroath engine-

house, poised half-way down the cliffside.

ST AUSTELL
MAP REF: 92SX0152

This busy town became the capital of the china clay country last century. Today its narrow streets and alleyways merge with modern shopping precincts and undercover markets. All the streets radiate from the delicately-carved 15th-century tower of Holy Trinity Church. Its original waggon roof is worth inspection, as is the magnificently timbered roof of the large Market Hall opposite. There are numerous interesting old inns, the most notable being the White Hart Hotel.

Those unique white pyramids of china clay sand-spoil which dominate the landscape north of the town are sometimes known as the Cornish Alps. It was William Cookworthy who first discovered large deposits of china clay or kaolin in Cornwall in 1755. Originally used for making porcelain, it is now used for coating

◀ Wheal Coates, south of St Agnes Head

paper and in the manufacture of house-paint, some medicines and numerous other items. The massive industry that developed made Britain the world's leading exporter of china clay, most being shipped from Fowey, Par and Charlestown. The giant firm of English China Clays are presently landscaping and planting grass on many of the white spoil-heaps to make them less obtrusive.

Almost every one of the grey granite communities of the clay area, together with many other Cornish villages, boasts its own silver band, and each year they exhibit their prowess at a festival in the aptly-named village of Bugle.

A display of china clay industry artefacts, equipment, clothes and locomotives can be seen at the Wheal Martyn Museum, a 19th-century clay-works situated in a deep, wooded valley at Carthew two miles north of St Austell on the Bodmin road. Also north of St Austell is the village of Roche with its attendant Roche Rock, an impressive and unique outcrop of altered granite rising to a high point of 60ft. Built into the rock is a 14th-century chapel.

SAINTS

Cornwall, it is said, boasts more saints than were ever enthroned in heaven. Certainly, when St Augustine arrived in Kent in AD597 to convert the heathen English, the faith was already burning bright in Cornwall.

For a hundred years Celtic missionaries had been arriving on its shores from Wales and Ireland, converting small groups of people to Christianity. They were encouraged by their own

▼ A survivor of Cornwall's Celtic Church

monasteries to make these pilgrimages overseas to convert and teach the heathen populace, founding a 'cell' or church before moving on to continue their work. Most established their cells near sites where the people had been accustomed to worshipping – springs, wells, rivers or standing stones. Many lived as contemplative hermits, adhering to a strict ascetic code. Many were never 'sainted' in an ecclesiastical sense, but their names live on in the dedications of over 200 old Cornish churches and even more villages and towns.

The first wave of saints arrived in the 5th century, and the effect of these simple, ragged, wonder-working proselytisers on small communities must have been quite startling. Legends of their lives and powers abounded. St Brychan, it is said, arrived from Wales with three wives, 12 sons and 12 daughters, including Endellion, Issey, Kew, Mabyn, Minver and Teath, all of whom became saints. St Keyne is supposed to have arrived on a mill-stone, St Budoc in a barrel and several Breton saints floating on their stone altars. St Fingar (Gwinear) arrived from Ireland with his brothers St Breaca (Breage), St Euny (Lelant) and St Erc (Erth). Their sister Ia (Ives) arrived separately, floating on an ivy leaf.

St Piran, patron saint of tinners, is said to have had a taste for the bottle, while saints Keverne and Just gained a reputation for being aggressive rivals. A strange mixture of the old and new religions forms a part of many legends concerning battles between the saints and the old Cornish giants. The saints usually won these boulder-throwing contests, thanks to heavenly intervention.

Bizarre legends apart, the success of the missionary work carried out by these Irish, Welsh and Breton saints was genuine enough and local kings and chieftains readily gave large areas of land for the building of monasteries and colleges. The most influential saint was undoubtedly St Petroc, who travelled from Wales to found monasteries in Padstow and Bodmin, also visiting Devon, Somerset and Brittany. Another Welsh saint, Sampson, Christianized a stone pillar being worshipped by heathens by carving a cross on its side. Many such Celtic crosses, carved by or dedicated to the early saints, can be seen in Cornish churchyards. The memory of these good men and women also lives on in the annual Feast Days held in most villages and towns in Cornwall today.

may have been required for processions or as a carriageway at a time when other buildings crowded in from the west. Attempts at damp-proofing the tower with rendering have marred its style. Yet the church is delightfully placed and flanked on its south and east prospects by attractive old houses, like a cathedral close. The town itself has a fine medieval feel to it with tall slate-hung buildings flanking narrow wynds and connecting alleyways.

A former landlord of the Red Lion Inn was James Polkinghorne, a champion in the art of Cornish wrestling. The name of another inn, the Silver Ball, refers to the small silver-coated wooden ball for which two teams battle fiercely every Shrove Tuesday and second Saturday following. The object of these hurling matches is to carry the ball to one of two goals which are two miles apart. The hurling is played between 'Town' and 'Country' and is of great antiquity, having been common in

ST BURYAN
MAP REF: 90SW4025

St Buryan lies at the centre of the more pastoral southern half of the Land's End Peninsula. It is an attractive village with a splendid church whose four-staged tower is still used as a convenient landmark even by high-tech fishermen coming into Mount's Bay from the south. In the dark interior of the church is a wide rood-screen carved with hunting scenes, strange beasts and vine leaves.

About one mile north of St Buryan is the well-preserved late Neolithic stone circle of Boscawen-Un with its 19 stones and leaning central pillar. Dating from about 5,000 years ago this is a major ancient monument. The first meeting of the Gorsedd of the Bards of Cornwall was held at Boscawen-Un in 1928.

ST CLEER
MAP REF: 92SX2468

This compact group of moorstone cottages surrounding a stout-walled 15th-century church, lies on the south-west fringe of Bodmin Moor, close to a former quarrying and mining area. St Cleer church has an intriguing Victorian stained glass window depicting eleven female saints. Down the road past the village

▲ Detail of the fine carved rood-screen in St Buryan's church

inn is the rather Gothic-looking open-sided chapel built over St Cleer's Well and now surrounded by modern houses. In a field north-east of the village stands Trethevy Quoit, an impressive Neolithic chamber tomb with a massive capstone.

Alongside a road north-west of the village is the Doniert Stone, a block of granite carved with intricate designs and dedicated to a 9th-century Cornish king who drowned nearby. Turn north at Redgate to reach an ancient packhorse bridge, from where a footpath leads along the wooded banks of the River Fowey to Golitha Falls.

A short drive north of St Cleer is Siblyback Lake, a reservoir where visitors can sail, windsurf or fish for brown or rainbow trout with a day permit. A Visitor Centre contains a café and geological display.

ST COLUMB MAJOR
MAP REF: 91SW9163

At the head of the Vale of Lanherne, the little market town of St Columb Major was considered as the site for Cornwall's cathedral, but lost the battle to more centrally-placed Truro. The fine tower of St Columba's church has a through-arch which

JOHN WESLEY

Poverty, violence and a contempt for the law were common amongst the hard-drinking, wild-living members of Cornwall's 18th-century mining and fishing communities. The Church offered little personal contact, seeming instead to be the province of the mine-owners and landed gentry.

When the preacher John Wesley made the first of over 30 visits to Cornwall, in 1743, he was met with suspicion and opposition. On several occasions his life was put in danger when he was pelted with stones and attacked by hounds. After several visits, however, his courage was acknowledged and his simple, personal message was gradually accepted. Travelling on horseback, he visited towns and villages from Launceston to St Just, Polperro to St Ives, preaching first at small meetings in houses and cottages, and later at large open-air gatherings. The fiery preaching and passionate singing caused many conversions to Methodism and numerous places of worship were built throughout the county. These small 'bethels', chapels and churches were simple in design, often resembling the familiar mine buildings that

many parts of Cornwall in the past. Now it is staged only at St Ives and St Columb. The St Ives hurling is a pale remnant of a more vigorous tradition, but St Columb keeps the custom alive with spirit. Windows are barricaded on the evening of the hurling and the event is like some marvellously eccentric rugby match.

ST DAY
MAP REF: 91SW7342

Surrounded by the brick-topped chimneys of abandoned engine-houses, St Day preceded Redruth as the mining capital of Cornwall. Its terraces of miners' cottages and mine-captains' villas were once familiar to the evangelist John Wesley, who visited the town on numerous occasions. At nearby Busveal a deep hollow, Gwennap Pit, became a regular venue on his tours of Cornwall and now Methodists from all over the world have made it a place of pilgrimage.

surrounded the towns. Some of the journeys on horseback undertaken by Wesley in all weathers were gruelling, and special accommodation was provided for him at Trewint, near Altarnun, at St Just-in-Penwith and at Crantock. On one visit he preached six sermons and rode over 50 miles in three days.

Many of Wesley's best-attended meetings were held at Gwennap Pit, a hollow in the ground near St Day, converted by miners into an amphitheatre capable of holding several thousand people. Methodists still congregate here in large numbers for the annual Whit Monday service and to visit the adjacent memorial chapel. At the nearby mining village of Carharrack a small Museum of Cornish Methodism has been created in the church, which still contains its original box-pews and gaslights.

Since Wesley's death in 1791, the Methodists have split into several sects: Wesleyan; Bible Christians (or Bryonites); Primitive Methodists; United Methodist Free Church and Methodist New Connection. So powerful is the legacy left by John Wesley that many towns and villages contain chapels or churches to two, or even three of these sects.

◀ John Wesley, founder of Methodism, who rode about the country for 50 years preaching the gospel, often in the open air

ST EWE
MAP REF: 92SW9746

This attractive little village on the side of the River Luney valley, west of Mevagissey, contains some charming cottages and a 14th-century church surrounded by trees. Its spire is octagonal in shape and carvings of faces peering through foliage surround the doorway. The village stocks are now kept inside the church.

The rood-screen in St Ewe's is unique in that it is the only one of its age and style that survived the destructive zeal of Cromwell's soldiers. Outside the north porch is the St Ewe camellia, a variety bred at Caerhays Castle which lies on the coast three miles to the south.

In the wooded valley below the church is the hamlet of Polmassick, where you may taste wine made from locally-grown grapes and inspect delightful miniature ponies at Polmassick Vineyard.

▲ A magnificent Norman doorway with receding arches, at St German's church

ST GERMANS
MAP REF: 93SX3557

Built on a high spur at the confluence of two rivers, this charming village contains numerous attractive buildings with well-tended gardens. A row of balconied almshouses, built in 1538, has been carefully restored.

An Augustinian priory was established here in 1162, and its magnificent priory church was the chief church in Cornwall until the completion of Truro Cathedral in 1910. Rising on either side of its deep, carved doorway are two towers, dating from the 13th and 15th centuries. The spacious interior contains many memorials to the Eliot family whose home, Port Eliot, stands alongside the church, looking out over wooded parkland. A steep lane descends to the once-busy Victorian wharfs at St Germans Quay. Just south of St Germans at the western end of Whitsand Bay is Portwrinkle, a small cove known for its hardy breed of small-boat fishermen. The remains of the storm-battered, semi-circular harbour can still be seen. When caught at sea in very bad storms the Portwrinkle fishermen of old could not risk landing at home. Instead they would sail up Plymouth Sound and the River Lynher to St Germans and then drag their boats to Portwrinkle.

◀ Grapes ripening on the vine at Polmassick Vineyard near St Ewe

ST IVES
MAP REF: 90SW5140

The magnificent golden beaches of St Ives cater for everyone from safe family sunbathing at Porthminster, The Harbour, and Porthgwidden Beaches to invigorating surf at Blue Flag Porthmeor Beach. Yet St Ives is famous for its connections with the Arts as well as its excellence as a holiday venue. It has great historical significance as an ancient borough and as one of the major centres of the pilchard fishing industry up until the early years of this century. One day in 1868 a record catch of 16½ million fish were caught in one seine net off St Ives. Pilchards were piled into mounds and pressed to release blood and oil. They were then salted and packed tightly into hogshead for export to the Mediterranean countries where strict Catholicism guaranteed numerous meatless fast days. The wealth-earning pilchards' blood and oil stained the streets of the town, and filled the air with the kind of reek that would drive away today's tourists in shoals.

As well as pilchards, tin and copper ore from surrounding mines was exported and the golden beaches of the town were once black with the dust from imported coal. The main arm of the harbour is Smeaton's Pier, built by the famous architect of the Eddystone Light.

The maze of streets behind the wharf is divided into 'Downalong', the abode of the fishing community, and 'Upalong', where the mining families lived. There was little love between the two and much fighting between rival gangs of youngsters in the old days. There are no mines or miners left now and the fishing fleet is greatly reduced, but St Ives still has several impeccably kept fishing boats and boasts a fine modern lifeboat. The piercing shrieks of gulls echo in cobbled alleyways and flowery courtyards, and steep streets of whitewashed cottages bear such names as Rope Walk, Mount Zion, Virgin Street and Fish Street. The finest cottages, many with outside staircases, can be found in a lane called The Digey at the foot of which is the old artist's and fishermen's inn, The Sloop. John Wesley's frequent visits to the town, as well as the firm grip of Methodism, are recalled in the names of Salubrious Street and Teetotal Street. At the foot of the town, by West Pier, rises the golden tower of the parish church, dedicated to St Ia, a 6th-century female missionary who is said to have arrived here from Ireland floating on an ivy leaf. The church contains a fine barrel roof and a tender sculpture of Our Lady and Child by Barbara Hepworth.

St Ives became the haunt of artists following a visit by the painter Turner in the 1880s. Sickert and Whistler worked here, attracted by the clear light, and many others followed in their wake. As the fishing industry declined, so net-lofts and fish cellars were converted into studios. Ben Nicholson and Peter Lanyon headed a new wave this century, together with Barbara Hepworth. Examples of her work can be seen in a delightful garden setting at the Barbara Hepworth Museum in Back Street. The potter Bernard Leach started the Leach Pottery at Higher Stennack; and many artists still work in or near the town. A specially built art gallery above Porthmeor Beach is scheduled for completion in 1992.

A narrow lane of old houses known as The Warren meanders behind the rocky headland of Pedn Olva to Porthminster and the railway station. The train ride into St Ives from the main line at St Erth is one of the finest branch line journeys in Britain. It skirts the bird sanctuary of Lelant Saltings and reveals the vista of St Ives Bay with breathtaking

suddenness. Running east from St Ives towards Lelant and Hayle is the more modern resort of Carbis Bay above a delightful beach which maintains the overall Mediterranean ambience of the area.

ST JUST
MAP REF: 90SW3731

The most westerly town in mainland England, St Just bustled with activity last century when nearby tin and copper mines were in full production. Its streets of gabled, grey-granite houses and old inns still have a busy working atmosphere despite there being no working mines left in the district. Two imposing Methodist churches, one with a Doric façade, and a sturdy 15th-century church dominate the low-roofed town. At its centre is an ancient Plain-an-Gwarry or 'Playing Place', a grass-covered amphitheatre where medieval miracle or mystery plays were once performed.

West of St Just is the impressive headland of Cape Cornwall, now in the care of the National Trust. Always noted as the 'only cape in England', the distinction is rarely explained. A cape is a headland at the meeting of two oceans or channels. Cape Cornwall was known as the ancient Land's End because it was believed to be at the meeting of the English Channel and St George's Channel. Offshore lie The Brisons, rocks notoriously dangerous to shipping in the past and reputed to have once been used as a particularly grim open-air prison.

The coast from the Cape area to the north is one of the most astonishing

▼ Looking across to St Ives, once Cornwall's main pilchard fishing port

its lighthouse, built in 1834. The now defunct St Anthony Battery is also sited here. Built in 1904 it was still fully operational in 1956. It was one of many such coastal batteries erected before World War I when ports like Falmouth were considered vulnerable in a volatile European world.

ST KEVERNE
MAP REF: 91SW7921

Although built a mile or so inland from the coast, the tower and octagonal steeple of St Keverne Church act as a day-mark to sailors, helping them stay clear of the baleful group of offshore rocks known as The Manacles on the approach to Helford and Falmouth Bay. In the churchyard are the tombstones of over 400 men who have perished along this stretch of coast. Radiating from a small square, the village is often swept by fierce gale-force winds which whip across the high Lizard plateau. It was a St Keverne blacksmith, Joseph An Gof (Michael Joseph) who, together with Thomas Flamank of Bodmin, led an ill-fated march to London in 1497 against a punitive tax being levied by Henry VII to fund his war in Scotland. Both were hanged at Tyburn.

To the north and east of St Keverne are the villages of Porthoustock and Porthallow, pronounced 'P'rewstock' and 'P'raller'. Originally fishing communities, they are now devoted to roadstone quarrying.

areas of industrial archaeology in Britain. Here were the famous coastal mines of West Cornwall: in the Kenidjack Valley, at Levant, The Crowns at Botallack and the modern Geevor, now sadly closed.

From the hamlet of Botallack, ¾ mile north of St Just, a track leads to the cliff-top from where you can look down on the recently restored Crown engine-houses of Botallack mine. The shaft of this old mine sloped down under the sea and on stormy nights miners could hear the sound of boulders shifting on the sea-bed above them.

ST JUST IN ROSELAND
MAP REF: 91SW8435

The Roseland Peninsula is a small paradise with woodlands and sheltered creeks to the north-west and rocky cliffs to the south-east. Running down its centre is the winding Percuil River. The peninsula is renowned for its beauty, but nowhere is it more luxuriant than at St Just In Roseland, where a small 13th- and 15th-century church stands on the water's edge at the head of a wooded tidal creek. Behind rises a hillside churchyard of semi-tropical trees and shrubs, a blaze of colour in early summer. Across the peninsula is the fishing village of Portscatho which still supports a small boat fishery, chiefly for shellfish. Near the southern tip of the peninsula, a wooded lane leads down to St Anthony and a small church standing alongside Place House, former home of the Spry family. Beyond here an old military road runs down to St Anthony Head with

▲ A fisherman unloading his catch beside the harbour at St Ives

◄ The cliff-side mines at Botallack near St Just

▼ The beautiful creek-side setting of St Just In Roseland's church

ST MAWES
MAP REF: 91SW8433

A sunny hillside of white houses and villas rises from the harbour of St Mawes, now a popular yachting haven. Its steep lanes contain many charming old cottages overhung with flowers. At the mouth of the Percuil River to the west stands St Mawes Castle, built by Henry VIII in 1542 to protect the ports of Truro and Falmouth. It was built to the same 'clover-leaf' design as the much larger Pendennis Castle across the mouth of Carrick Roads. Its dungeons, barrack rooms and cannon-lined walls are open to the public.

ST MAWGAN
MAP REF: 91SW8765

Surrounded by woodland in the deep, sheltered Vale of Lanherne, this picturesque village consists of charming cottages, the old Falcon Inn, a turret-towered church and a pair of bridges spanning a slow-moving stream. The 13th-century manor house of the Arundell family has been the convent of a closed order of nuns since 1794. A remarkably carved lantern-cross dating from 1420 stands in the churchyard, near to a boat-shaped wooden memorial recording the fate of nine men and a boy who froze in their lifeboat after a shipwreck in 1846.

At the foot of the Vale is the sheltered sandy cove of Mawgan Porth, and a mile to the north are Bedruthan Steps, owned by the National Trust – high outcrops of rock on a flat sandy beach. Said to be the stepping-stones of the Cornish giant Bedruthan, a more prosaic explanation for the 'steps' is that they relate to the original cliffside staircase down to the beach built at least as early as the beginning of last century. In 1990 hard winter weather caused further weakening of the friable rock faces above the modern concrete staircase. To date (1991), the Trust has been forced to close off access to the beach because of extreme danger to the public, although possibilities for safe access are being investigated.

ST MERRYN
MAP REF: 94SW8874

Cottages cluster around the Church of St Marina in this tiny village of grey slate. To the west Trevose Head juts out into the Atlantic, a lighthouse at its tip. Padstow lifeboat is based on its sheltered eastern side in Mother Ivey's Bay. This popular family beach is divided from another safe beach at Harlyn Bay by Cataclews Point, where much of the blue-grey greenstone used to make church fonts and window tracery was quarried. On the western side of Trevose head, below a superbly-sited golf course, are the beaches of Booby's Bay and Constantine Bay where there is good surfing for the expert.

ST MICHAEL'S MOUNT
MAP REF: 90SW5129

The grandeur of St Michael's Mount and its glorious setting in the north-east corner of Mount's Bay has made it a place of pilgrimage since the Middle Ages. Today about half a million people a year either walk across the cobbled causeway at low tide or use one of the small ferries that ply between the Mount and Marazion on the mainland. It is probable that the Mount was once a land-locked hill surrounded by marshy woodland before the sea encroached. Relics of a petrified forest have been found in the surrounding waters.

▲ The 14th-century church tower dominates the village of St Neot

The small harbour at the foot of the Mount is thought to be the site of Ictis, from where tin was shipped to the Mediterranean during the Iron Age. An inshore lifeboat is now based at the harbour.

In 495 the archangel St Michael was said to have appeared to a group of fishermen on the seaward side of the Mount, thus guaranteeing its sanctity and fame for ever. Edward the Confessor granted the Mount to the Benedictine's of Mont St Michel in Normandy, and in 1135 a priory was founded on its summit. Henry V seized the Mount during the war with France and in 1424 granted the

priory to the Abbey of Syon at Twickenham. It was at this time that the harbour and causeway were built. Henry VIII appropriated the Mount on the Dissolution of the Monasteries in 1535 and it became a fortress. The Mount was a Royalist stronghold during the 17th-century Civil War, but fell to the Parliamentary forces and was placed under the command of Colonel John St Aubyn who bought it in 1659 and whose descendant Lord St Levan still lives in the castle. Lord St Levan presented the Mount to the National Trust in 1954. The Mount, together with a large part of the castle and its environs is open to the public.

▶ Medieval stained glass in the church at St Neot

▼ Walking across the cobbled cause way to St Michael's Mount at low tide

ST NEOT

MAP REF: 92SX1867

Formerly a centre for wool and locally-mined tin and slate, this quiet village is tucked away in a deep, wooded hollow on the edge of Bodmin Moor. Water which began life in the mysterious Dozmary Pool rushes under a stone bridge beside a friendly old inn. St Neot's church contains some of the most magnificent medieval stained glass in England. There are 15 windows with about half of the glass being of great antiquity. On a day of changing light the full beauty of the subtle cast of colours on the inside of the church can be best appreciated.

St Neot was only 4ft tall. He lived upstream from the church by a pool which miraculously always contained two fish. He was only allowed to eat one at a time, and when his servant accidentally caught and cooked both fish, the good Neot threw one back into the pool where it returned to life.

A couple of miles to the west, steep moorland lanes lead up to the remote hamlet of Warleggan. Here lived the eccentric Revd Frederick Densham, who became parish priest in 1931. Disliked by his parishioners, he surrounded the rectory with a high wall and withdrew from the world. Lacking a Sunday congregation, the priest preached to a group of cards propped in the pews, each one bearing a name. He died alone in the rectory in 1953.

North of St Neot lies Colliford Lake Reservoir where there is a Country Park with rare breeds.

SALTASH
MAP REF: 93SX4258

The original link between Saltash and Plymouth was provided by a small ferry which crossed the Tamar from the Passage Inn. Isambard Kingdom Brunel's magnificent iron single-track railway bridge was opened by Prince Albert in 1859 and a road link was provided by the three-lane suspension bridge in 1961.

Saltash was an ancient port used for exporting tin from Dartmoor. It was eclipsed by Plymouth but continued to hold symbolic control over the entire Tamar estuary until the early 19th century. The old waterside area of Saltash is no more but the contrast of the surviving 16th-century and late 17th- and 18th-century houses and the great granite piers of Brunel's Prince Albert Bridge is striking. The steep streets of the old town contain many fine buildings, and in Culver Street is Mary Newman's Cottage, where the first wife of Sir Francis Drake was born. In the town centre is a 17th-century pillared guildhall, now used for markets, and the parish church with an unusual 17th-century clock in its slate tower. The leafy lanes and creeks north of Saltash are worth exploring.

SANCREED
MAP REF: 90SW4229

This attractive little village lies at the heart of the Land's End Peninsula. It is the only parish in the immediate district without a coastline, but the sea is dramatically visible from its moorland heights. The 15th-century church is in a delightful leafy setting. Its rood-screen has some lively carvings and there are two splendid crosses in the churchyard.

Sancreed Beacon is a fine rounded hill above the village. Further west is the Iron Age hill-fort of Caer Bran, reached by a footpath from the

▲ Spanning the Tamar at Saltash. Brunel's Prince Albert Bridge, in the foreground

delightfully named hamlet of Grumbla a mile west of Sancreed. Half a mile west from here is the beautifully preserved Iron Age courtyard village of Carn Euny with its striking *fogou*, a long enclosed tunnel-chamber. Carn Euny can be reached from Sancreed through the hamlet of Brane.

SEATON
MAP REF: 93SX3254

The long sheltered coastline fringing Whitsand Bay between Looe and Nare Head has a number of beaches. Seaton and its neighbour Downderry both have safe, easily accessible beaches and good car parking. This was a lonely and remote coast last

century in an area notorious for smuggling. There were strong local links with Brittany from where luxury goods like brandy, silk and spices were brought ashore at numerous points along the coast. At times the smugglers would apply their existing skills as fishermen by sinking sealed brandy kegs, attached to a weighted line and secured at either end with anchors, to be retrieved later by grapnel.

The Monkey Sanctuary at Murraytown lies a mile to the east and has the first protected breeding colony of Amazonian Woolly monkeys in the world.

SENNEN
MAP REF: 90SW3525

Sennen is in two distinct parts; the village of Sennen on the flat plateau of Land's End, and Sennen Cove – flanked by Whitesand Bay and the adjoining Gwenver Beach, one of the finest surfing beaches in the country. Near Sennen Cove harbour is a splendid wooden round-house which contained the rope and chain windlass for hauling boats clear of the sea.

Lifeboats at Sennen have given outstanding service since 1853 round the notorious Land's End. A fine modern vessel is still stationed there.

West of Sennen Cove is Pedn-men-du headland and Maen Castle, a fine example of an Iron Age cliff castle.

◀ The broad, sandy expanse of beach at Sennen Cove

TINTAGEL
MAP REF: 94SX0588

Tintagel owes its 'Arthurian industry' to Alfred Lord Tennyson who visited in the 1840s and was inspired to write *Morte d'Arthur* and the later *Idylls of the King*. Visits by Dickens, Thackeray and Swinburne ensured the area's fame as a tourist centre, and North Cornwall Railway did the rest.

The great headland of Tintagel has had a powerful history. Whether or not there was a Celtic settlement on the headland is disputed although archaeological investigations continue. The headland was a possible trading centre pre-Norman Conquest and the surviving castle was built during the 12th and 13th-centuries. There are also traces of medieval field systems. The spirit of King Arthur dominates and finds full expression at the Hall of Chivalry and King Arthur's Hall built by an Arthurian devotee. There are 73 stained glass windows displaying heraldry of the Knights of the Round Table and many other exhibits. Within the village, the 14th century building now known as the Old Post Office is a delight, it seems to happily grow out of the ground. Originally a small medieval manor house, the building was used as a post office last

▲ The weathered cliffs and dark caves are all part of the wild appeal of the coast at Tintagel; legendary birthplace of King Arthur

century and is now in the care of the National Trust.

The coast to the south of Tintagel Head was a hive of Victorian industry, with slate being quarried from the sea cliffs and cliff tops, and off-loaded down sheer cliffs at Penhallick Point on to sailing vessels. Along the coast north-east of Tintagel, a stream gushes down a woody glen from St Nectan's Kieve, home of a Celtic hermit, past an old mill to meet the sea in Rocky Valley.

North-east of Sennen is Land's End Airport, from where short flights can be taken along the coast and from where an air service links with the Isles of Scilly.

▼ Tintagel's rare medieval slate manor house, the Old Post Office

LANGUAGE AND TRADITIONS

Remote and unaffected by the Roman Conquest, Cornwall was a Celtic country whose strongest links were overseas. Its people were first cousins to the Welsh and Bretons and second cousins to the Scots, Irish and Manx. Until the 18th century it had a language of its own, similar to those of the other Celtic nations: Iron Age tribes introduced the Brythonic branch of the language to Cornwall, and its similarities with the other Celtic languages can be found:

English	river	island	sweet
Cornish	avon	enys	melys
Welsh	avon	ynys	milis
Breton	avon	enez	melys
Irish	abbahn	inis	milis
Scottish			
Gaelic	abhainn	innis	milis
Manx	awin	innys	millish

A local rhyme states:
  By Tre, Pol and Pen,
  Ye shall know Cornishmen'

▲ Dolly Pentreath, Mousehole fishwife and the last person to speak only Cornish

and a quick glance at any map or telephone directory will show an abundance of names beginning with the prefixes Tre (a homestead or hamlet), Pol (a pool or pond) and Pen (chief, a headland or hill). Many poems and plays written during the golden age of the Cornish language in the 14th and 15th centuries have survived, but the imposition of Anglicanism and strengthening links with England caused a steady decline in the language. Only in the far west was it kept alive until the death in 1777 of Dolly Pentreath, a fisherwoman from Mousehole who was reputed to be the last monoglot Cornish-speaker.

Recently there has been a resurgence of interest in the ancient tongue and it is now taught at evening classes and in some local schools.

A ceremony held entirely in Cornish is the annual Gorsedd of the Bards of Kernow (Cornwall), held on the first Saturday in September at some historic site. Similar in style to the Welsh and Breton Gorsedds, this colourful event is part prize-giving to the writers of poems and songs in Cornish, and part rejoicing in Celtic tradition.

Many other Cornish customs and traditions have their roots in the dim Celtic past. The ancient custom of hurling is kept alive in St Ives and St Columb Major, while the sport of Cornish wrestling is still a popular summer event in Cornwall and Brittany. Padstow's 'Obby 'Oss is led by a 'teazer' through the streets of Padstow on May Day, and the ancient 'Hal-an-Tow' mumming play precedes the Flora Day dances at Helston on 8th May.

TORPOINT

TORPOINT

MAP REF: 93SX4355

Until the opening of the road bridge at Saltash in 1961, the car-ferry linking Torpoint with Devonport and Plymouth was one of the leading 'gateways' to Cornwall. Shipbuilding and repairing were the industries here, and this small working town retains strong links with the naval dockyard across the water. The Torpoint ferry still regularly crosses the Hamoaze on the Plymouth commuter run.

The National Trust property of Antony House, a splendid example of

◄ Mount Edgecumbe House; originally built in the 16th century and gutted during World War II, the more recent building is surrounded by beautiful grounds

a Queen Anne mansion lying about two miles north-west of Torpoint, is surrounded by thickly-wooded gardens and lawns sloping down to the riverside. The Carew family have lived on this estate since the 15th century, and the present house, built in 1721 is of Georgian elegance, comprising grey stone facing a forecourt enclosed by colonnades, and with east and west wings of red brick. The house contains exquisite tapestries, a large library and dining room and some fine pieces of 18th-century furniture. In the village church of Antony, a couple of miles to the west, is a splendid full-length brass of Lady Margery Arundell dating from 1420.

TREGONY
MAP REF: 91SW9244

In medieval times large ships sailed up the River Fal to this port, to collect hides and unload limestone

▼ The gardens of Trelissick which overlook the River Fal are best visited in the spring and early summer

▲ Looking down the main street of the quiet village of Tregony, once a busy medieval port

and coal. Market produce from the Roseland Peninsula was sold here and until 1832 it sent two MPs to Westminster. As the river became clogged with silt, so Tregony's importance declined, and it is now a quiet village where the pace of life is slow. In the steep main street are a row of balconied almshouses, dating from 1696 but rebuilt in 1895, and a Gothic clock-tower.

TRELISSICK
MAP REF: 91SW8339

The National Trust gardens of Trelissick overlook the beautiful River Fal. Extensive park and woodlands surround a large garden of flowering shrubs, best seen in the spring and early summer. The elegant 19th-century house with its Grecian façade is not open to the public, but there is a National Trust shop and a restaurant in the old stable block. There is a delightful woodland walk round Trelissick's splendid grounds and alongside the River Fal. All is beautifully described in a special leaflet.

The King Harry Ferry provides a close-up view of the deep sea vessels which often lie-up in the sheltered waters. There was probably a ferry here prior to the Norman Conquest. The name King Harry is believed to refer to King Henry VI.

Beside the road from Trelissick, west to Carnon Downs, stands the thatched Quaker meeting-house of Come-to-Good. Built in 1710, this charming whitewashed building has small latticed windows and a thatched stable. Its name stems from the Cornish words for 'House in the wooded combe'.

TRESILLIAN
MAP REF: 91SW8646

The Tresillian River is the northern branch of the Truro River. At the junction of the two is Malpas, site of an ancient ferry and a noted shipbuilding centre for schooners, ketches, barges and steamships. Tresillian lies nearly three miles upstream and was once the head of navigation and the lowest bridging point on the river. It had its moment of fame in 1646 when negotiations between Parliamentary and Royalist forces on the bridge led to the signing of a cease-fire in the Civil War. The Parliamentary army had their headquarters at the Wheel Inn, which has a spoked wheel made of straw on its thatched roof. On the opposite bank is a charming lodge entrance to the Tregothnan estate and mansion, home of Lord Falmouth. Tregothnan is not open to the public.

TRURO

MAP REF: 91SW8244

Cornwall's cathedral city and centre of business and administration, Truro has added to its stature with the opening of the new Crown Court; an award-winning modern building. The Court was previously at Bodmin.

Truro grew as an inland seaport in the Middle Ages. Well protected from direct attack by sea, it became a prosperous market and stannary town, ore from local mines being shipped from its wharfs. Mine waste and silt slowly clogged the higher reaches of the Truro River, and by the late 17th century, the town was in decline. Truro's revival and virtual rebuilding came during the 18th century when the high price paid for tin and copper caused an expansion in the mining industry. Wealthy merchants and banks moved to the town, and several important local families built town houses. The 19th century saw Truro in the ascendant as an elegant Georgian town considered to be the 'London of the West'. The main turnpike roads all led to Truro, which rapidly became the commercial heart of Cornwall's remarkable Victorian industrial era. The arrival of the railway in 1859 put Truro firmly on the map. It gained its city status in 1877 and the completion of the cathedral in 1910 made it the focus of social and business life.

▲ Truro Cathedral, whose foundation stone was laid in 1880 by the future Edward VII, was completed in 1910

Today Truro is a busy, spacious shopping city with much new development in the city centre. The main quay was filled in some years ago, and very little shipping now navigates the narrow approach to Truro's wharfs. The three-spired cathedral, one of the few to be completed in Britain this century and the first to be constructed for 800 years, is built of granite and Bath stone in Gothic and Early English styles. It was built on the site of the existing 16th-century Parish Church of St Mary, which the architect John L Pearson incorporated into the cathedral's south wall, enriching the building with its wonderfully ornate early 16th-century style. The interior of the main cathedral is rather clean-cut and austere, although spacious and elegant and beautifully vaulted. The baptistry in the south transept – with its pillars of Bath and Polyphant stone, exquisite vaulting, Breccio marble font and oak canopy – is particularly splendid.

The general architecture of Truro is impressive. The Georgian Assembly Rooms and Theatre in Pydar Street were at the centre of the town's social life in the 1800s. On the south side of Boscawen Street is the imposing City Hall, behind which is situated the indoor Pannier Market. The wide street rising steeply to the south of the city is Lemon Street, lined with elegant Georgian houses and still one of the best preserved complete Georgian streets in England.

Running off Victoria Square is Walsingham Place, a delightful small crescent of Georgian houses. Truro is also a city of narrow alleyways or 'opes' with names like Squeezegutts Alley and Burton's Ope. Tippet's Backlet runs from High Cross through to River Street, where stands the Royal Institution of Cornwall and County Museum, with a superb collection of minerals, paintings by Cornish artists and displays of prehistoric and later finds.

VERYAN

MAP REF: 91SW9139

A tranquil village in a lush wooded hollow, Veryan is best known for its circular 19th-century round houses, each topped with a conical thatched roof and a cross. Their shape stems from an old tradition that the devil likes to hide and lie in wait in corners. Luxuriant trees and shrubs surround the church above a small water garden. A deep lane runs south-west from the village down to sandy Pendower Beach, a safe bathing place. East of Veryan, the fishing village of Portloe straggles down a long narrow inlet in the cliffs.

The road winding north-east from Veryan descends the high cliffs to the sandy cove of Portholland before looping inland to Tubb's Mill and returning to the coast at Porthluney Cove. Look inland from the flat sandy beach to see the battlements, towers and turrets of Caerhays Castle against a dark background of high trees.

◄ Veryan is well-known for its 19th-century round houses

▲ The Bridge on Wool which spans the River Camel at Wadebridge

WADEBRIDGE
MAP REF: 94SW9972

The 14-arch bridge of this ancient port, the lowest on the River Camel, is also the longest in Cornwall and originally had 17 spans. It is known as 'The Bridge on Wool', traditionally thought to mean that its 15th-century foundations were laid on wool-packs for stability. However, it seems more likely to refer to the money raised to pay for the bridge, which came mainly from wealthy sheep-farmers who wanted an easier passage across the river. The importance of the town grew when Wadebridge was linked to Bodmin by one of Britain's earliest railways in 1834, the line later being extended as far as Padstow. Wadebridge was an extremely busy port last century importing coal, timber, limestone and general goods while exporting salt, iron ore and china clay. The railway was closed in 1967, but the five-mile riverside stretch to Padstow now makes a pleasant scenic walk.

Today Wadebridge is a busy shopping centre serving a wide agricultural area. The Royal Cornwall Show is held here in June each year. Upstream and on the opposite bank is Egloshayle, a landing place even older than Wadebridge. A hillside of cottages with well-tended gardens climbs from an old inn and the riverside church.

ZENNOR
MAP REF: 90SW4538

The unspoilt stretch of north coast between St Ives and St Just is Celtic Cornwall at its finest, with rugged, boulder-strewn moorland topped by granite tors, sloping down to bracken-covered cliffs and the sea. Low farmhouses huddle close together in the brooding landscape of this wild and windswept coast and the basic pattern of the small irregular fields dates back to the Iron Age.

The village of Zennor is particularly lovely and has a history stretching back to the Early Bronze Age 4,000 years ago. The few houses are centred on the nicely placed church of St Senera. Opposite and at a suitably lower level is the handsome Tinner's Arms whose name reflects the inevitable mining activity of the past. Down the road from the pub is the charming Wayside Folk Museum, a cottage containing a traditional Cornish kitchen and an outdoor exhibition of domestic and mining implements. A narrow lane from the church leads down the lush valley to Pendour Cove and Zennor head, owned by the National Trust.

Zennor's enduring legend relates how a local squire's son and church chorister Matthew Trewhella was lured to his doom in the dark waters of Pendour Cove below Zennor Head by the singing of a beautiful mermaid. A handsome carved bench-end in the church depicts the rather un-Christian lass herself. Zennor has close links with a number of distinguished artists and writers including W.H. Hudson, and D.H. Lawrence who lived nearby for a short time during World War I. Zennor Hill above the village was used as a natural quarry last century and many of St Ives' houses were built of Zennor stone.

▼ Looking west along the coastline from Zennor Head, towards Pendour Cove, owned by the National Trust

◄ Home of the Edgecumbe family for centuries, some parts of Cotehele survive from the 14th century

PLACES TO VISIT

Places to visit in Cornwall are listed here under their nearest town or village, and where possible correspond to the entries in the gazetteer.

The details given are intended to provide a rough guide only to opening times. Very often a place may only be open for part of the day or close for lunch. Also, although stated as open all year, many places are closed over Christmas and New Year. Full information should be obtained in advance of a visit from a local tourist information centre (see Useful Information).

Many places are owned either by The National Trust or are in the care of English Heritage, and if this is the case the entry is accompanied by the abbreviation NT or EH.
BH = bank holiday
Etr = Easter

BODMIN

Bodmin Farm Park, Fletchersbridge. Open May to Sep, Mon to Sat.

Lanhydrock House (NT). *Magnificent house in wooded parkland.* Open end Mar to Oct, daily. House closed Mon, except BHs.

Pencarrow House, Washaway. *Georgian mansion set in 500 acres.* Open Etr to mid-Oct, Mon to Thu and Sun.

Regimental Museum, Victoria Barracks. *History of the Duke of Cornwall's Light Infantry.* Open all year, Mon to Fri. Closed BHs.

BOSCASTLE

Museum of Witchcraft. *Unusual exhibits connected with local folklore.* Open Etr to Oct, daily.

BREAGE

Godolphin House, Godolphin Cross. *Former home of the Earls of Godolphin.* Open May to Sep, at varying times, and BHs. Open during winter by appointment.

BUDE

Historical and Folk Exhibition, The Wharf. *Local history and folk items.* Open Etr to Oct, daily.

CALLINGTON

Ken Caro Garden, Pensilva. *Two acres with waterfowl and aviary.* Open May to Jun, Wed and Sun.

FACT FILE
CONTENTS

CALSTOCK

Cotehele House (NT). *House, gardens, watermill and maritime museum.* Open Apr to Oct, daily. House only closed Fri.

CAMBORNE

See **POOL**

CAMELFORD

Delabole Slate Quarry Museum. *History of slate industry and mining exhibits.* Open Etr to Nov, Mon to Fri.

North Cornwall Museum and Gallery, The Clease. *Displays include cobbling, dairywork, agriculture and quarrying.* Open Etr to Sep, Mon to Sat.

CHARLESTOWN

Charlestown Shipwreck and Heritage Museum. *Shipwreck, diving and local history displays.* Open Etr to Oct, daily.

CHYSAUSTER

Ancient Village (EH). *Iron Age settlement with underground chamber.* Open Apr to Sep, daily; Oct to Etr, Tue to Sun.

FALMOUTH

Maritime Museum, Custom House Quay. *Exhibits on board the tug St Denys.* Open Apr to Oct, daily.

Military Vehicle Museum, Lamanva. Open all year, daily.

Museum of Sailing Ships, Arts Centre. *Superb model boats.* Open all year, Mon to Fri.

Pendennis Castle (EH). *One of Henry VIII's many coastal forts.* Open Apr to Sep, daily; Oct to Etr, Tue to Sun.

FOWEY

Noah's Ark Folk Museum, Fore St. *Local folk items.* Open all year, Mon, Tue, Thu and Fri.

St Catherine's Castle (EH). *Ruined stronghold restored in 1855.* Open any reasonable time.

GOONHAVERN

World in Miniature, Bodmin Rd. *Theme park with famous landmarks in miniature plus lovely gardens.* Open Apr to Oct, daily.

GWEEK

Seal Sanctuary and Marine Rescue Centre. *A seal hospital with displays, aquarium and nature trails.* Open all year, daily.

▲ The beautiful formal gardens which surround Lanhydrock House

HAYLE

Paradise Park. *Tropical and rare birds.* Open all year, daily.

HELSTON

Flambard's Theme Park. *All-weather attractions of all kinds.* Open Etr to Oct, daily.

Helston Folk Museum, Old Butter Market. *Displays on the town and Lizard peninsula.* Open all year, Mon to Sat.

Poldark Mine, Wendron. *Tin mine with nine museums and film of Cornish mining.* Open Apr to Oct, daily.

LAND'S END

Land's End Experience. *Coastal walks, innovative exhibitions, coves.* Open all year, daily.

LANHYDROCK

see **BODMIN**

LANREATH

Farm and Folk Museum, Churchtown. *Farmhouse, dairy and farmyard exhibits. Demonstrations.* Open Etr to Oct, daily.

LAUNCESTON

Launceston Castle (EH). *Ruins dominate the town.* Open Apr to Sep, daily; Oct to Etr, Tue to Sun.

Launceston Steam Railway. *Round trip of three miles, and a motor and motorcycle museum.* Open Etr to Oct on certain days. Also Santa Specials.

Lawrence House Museum (NT). *Georgian house with local history displays.* Open Apr to Sep, Mon to Fri. Other times by appointment.

Tamar Otter Park and Wild Wood, North Petherwin. *Breeding colonies of otters, owls, pheasants and peacocks.* Open Apr to Oct, daily.

LISKEARD

Dobwalls Family Adventure Park. *Miniature American railroads and Adventureland.* Open Etr to Oct, daily; Nov to Etr at certain times.

Paul Corin Musical Collection, St Keyne. Open Etr, and May to Sep, daily.

Thornburn Museum and Gallery. *Paintings by wildlife artist Archibald Thorburn. Art and audio-visual displays of the countryside.* Open as Dobwalls.

▼ Pendennis Castle, one of a chain built as a defense against the French

▲ Restormel, one of Cornwall's finest castles, was begun in 1200

LOOE

Monkey Sanctuary, Murrayton. *Woolly monkeys in natural setting.* Open Etr; May to Sep, Sun to Thu.

LOSTWITHIEL

Restormel Castle (EH). *Well-preserved ruins and good views.* Open Etr to Sep, daily; Oct to Etr, Tue to Sun.

MADRON

Trengwainton Garden (NT). *Exotic trees and shrubs.* Open Mar to Oct, Wed to Sat and BH Mons.

MAWGAN

Trelowarren House and Chapel. House open Etr to Oct, Wed; Jul to Sep, Wed and Sun. Chapel open daily.

MAWNAN SMITH

Glendurgan Garden (NT). *Forty-acre wooded valley.* Open Mar to Oct, Tue to Sat and BH Mons.

Penjerrick Gardens. *Spring-flowering shrubs.* Open Mar to Sep, Wed and Sun.

MEVAGISSEY

Folk Museum, East Quay. *Fascinating items of port's history.* Open Etr to Sep, daily.

World of Model Railways, Meadow St. *Over 2,000 models and realistic layouts.* Open two weeks at Etr; May to Oct, daily (closed Oct half-term).

NEWQUAY

Dairyland, Tresillian Barton Summercourt. *Cows milked to music, and a countryside museum.* Open Etr to Oct, daily.

Holywell Bay Leisure Park. *Ponies, go-karts, roller-skating.* Open May to Sep, daily.

Newquay Zoo and Leisure Park, Trenance Park. Open Apr to Nov, daily.

Trerice (NT). *Elizabethan manor house with a museum of lawn mowers.* Open end Mar to Oct, Wed to Mon.

Tunnels Through Time, St Michael's Rd. *Legends of Cornwall brought to life with full-size characters.* Open Etr to Oct, daily.

PADSTOW

Prideaux Place. *Treasures, deer park, sunken garden and dairy.* Open Etr for two weeks, then end May to Sep, Sun to Thu.

Tropical Bird and Butterfly Gardens, Fentonluna La. *Free-flying in tropical house. Garden of sub-tropical plants.* Open all year, daily.

PENDEEN

see **ST JUST**

PENZANCE

Penlee House Museum and Art Gallery, Penlee Park. *History of the area and an exhibition of the Newlyn School of painting.* Open all year, Mon to Sat.

▼ The Country Life museum at Summercourt near Newquay

Royal Geological Society of Cornwall Museum, Alverton St. *Minerals and fossils.* Open May to Sep, Mon to Fri.

The Maritime Museum, Chapel St. *Treasures from shipwrecks and a warship.* Open Apr to Oct, Mon to Sat.

POLPERRO

Land of Legend and Model Village. *Cornish legend displays.* Open Etr to Oct, Sun to Fri.

Smugglers' Museum. *Colourful exhibits.* Open Apr to Oct, daily.

POOL

Camborne School of Mines Geological Museum. *Displays from Cornish mines and overseas.* Open all year, Mon to Fri.

Cornish Engines (NT), East Pool. *Relics of the tin-mining industry.* Open Apr to Oct, daily.

PROBUS

County Demonstration Garden. *Displays on many aspects of gardening.* Open May to Sep, daily; Oct to Apr, Mon to Fri.

Trewithen, Grampound Rd. *Internationally renowned landscape garden and small house.* House open Apr to Jul and Aug, BH Mon and Tue. Garden open Mar to Sep, Mon to Sat. Nurseries open all year.

ST AGNES

St Agnes Leisure Park. *Gardens, models and rides.* Open Etr to Oct, daily.

▼ Looking towards St Michael's Mount

St Agnes Museum. *Local History.* Open Etr to Sep, daily.

ST AUSTELL

Automobilia Motor Museum, St Stephen. *Vintage vehicles.* Open Apr to Sep, Tue to Sun; Oct to Mar, Sat and Sun.

Wheal Martyn Museum. *The story of china clay.* Open-air site. Open Apr to Oct, daily.

ST IVES

Barbara Hepworth Museum, Barnoon Hill. *Sculptures and personal effects in the artist's old home.* Open all year, Mon to Sat and Sun in Jul and Aug.

ST JUST

Geevor Tin Mine, Pendeen. *Models and history of mine.* Open Etr to Oct, daily.

▼ A Barbara Hepworth sculpture

The Levant Beam Engine (NT), Trewellard, Pendeen. *Oldest engine in Cornwall.* Open Etr to mid-Sep, Fri, Sun and BH Mons.

ST MAWES

St Mawes Castle (EH). *Fine example of military architecture with dungeons and barrack rooms.* Open Etr to Sep, daily; Oct to Etr, Tue to Sun.

ST MICHAEL'S MOUNT

Medieval castle (NT) reached by a causeway. Open end Mar to Oct, Mon to Fri and most weekends in season. Nov to Mar, guided tours only. Mar to May, educational visits by arrangement.

SANCREED

Carn Euny Ancient Village (EH). *First-century settlement.* Open any reasonable time.

TINTAGEL

Old Post Office (NT). *Fourteenth-century manor house.* Open Mar to Oct, daily.

Tintagel Castle (EH). *Romantic ruins on cliff edge.* Open Etr to Sep, daily; Oct to Etr, Tue to Sun.

TORPOINT

Antony House (NT). *Fine mansion with grounds overlooking river.* Open Apr to Oct, Tue to Thu and BH Mons. Also Sun, Jun to Aug.

Mount Edgcumbe Gardens. *Ornamental shrubberies and lawns.* House open Etr to Oct, daily. Park open all year, daily.

TREDINNICK

Cornish Shire Horse Centre, Trelow Farm. *Blacksmith, foals, carriages.* Open Etr to Oct, daily.

TRELISSICK

Trelissick Garden (NT). *Lovely wooded gardens with splendid views.* Open Mar to Oct, daily. Woodland walk open all year, daily.

TRERICE MANOR

see **NEWQUAY**

TRURO

Royal Cornwall Museum, River St. *Mineral collection, local paintings, archaeological finds.* Open all year, Mon to Sat, closed BHs.

WENDRON

see **HELSTON**

ZENNOR

Wayside Folk Museum. *Exhibits of Cornish village life.* Open mid-Mar to Oct, daily.

FACT FILE

SPORTS AND ACTIVITIES

The following information is by no means comprehensive and further details can be obtained from the authorities and contacts given.

Addresses are listed under Useful Information on page 83.

ANGLING

Day tickets for river fishing are available from local shops. Day tickets for course and game fishing at a number of reservoirs owned by South West Water Services Ltd are also available from self-service units. For further details contact South West Water.

Sea-fishing trips are available from the harbours at Falmouth, Looe, Mevagissey and Padstow.

BOAT TRIPS

Various cruises and boat trips are available from Falmouth, Fowey, Looe, Lostwithiel, Mevagissey, Newquay, Penzance, Polperro, St Ives and Truro during the season.

CYCLING

Bicycles can be hired at the following places.

Bodmin, *Bodmin Trading Co,* Church Square (0208 72557).

Camborne, *Aldridge Cycles,* 38 Cross Street (0209 714970).

▼ Fishing vessels moored up in Newquay's busy harbour

Falmouth, *Fraser-Paull,* 19 New Street (0326 312227).

Aldridge Cycles, 1 Swanpool Street (0326 318600).

Newquay, *Silly Cycles,* The Shop, Wesley Yard (0637 318600).

Penzance, *Penwith Cycles,* 51 Causeway Head (0736 62584).

The Cycle Centre, Knights Warehouse, Bread Street (0736 51671).

Geoff's Bikes, Victoria Palace (0736 63665).

Redruth, *Adams Cycles,* 57B West End (0209 212100).

Ricci Ltd, 82 Mount Ambrose (0209 215787).

Wadebridge, *Bridge Bike Hire,* Eddystone (020881 3050).

Bodmin Trading Company (020881 2021).

GOLF

The following clubs and courses welcome visitors.

Bude, *Bude and North Cornwall Golf Club,* Burn View (0288 352006).

Camborne, *Tehidy Park Golf Club,* 3m N of Camborne (0209 842208).

Constantine, *Trevose Golf Club,* Constantine Bay (0841 520208).

Falmouth, *Falmouth Golf Club,* Swanpool Road (0326 311262).

Launceston, *Launceston Golf Club,* St Stephens, 1m N of town centre (0566 3442).

Looe Bin Down Golf Club (0566 3442).

Lelant, *West Cornwall Golf Club,* (0736 753401).

Looe, *Looe Golf Club,* 3¹/₂m NE of Looe (05034 239).

Lostwithiel, *Lostwithiel Golf & Country Club,* Lower Polscoe (0208 873550).

Mawnan Smith, *Budock Vean Hotel,* 1¹/₂m SW of Mawnan Smith (0326 250288).

Mullion, *Mullion Golf Club,* Cury 1¹/₂m NW of Mullion (0326 240685).

Newquay, *Newquay Golf Club,* Tower Road (0637 872091).

Perranporth, *Perranporth,* Budnick Hill (0872 572454).

Portwrinkle, *Whitesand Bay Hotel* (0503 30276).

Praa Sands, *Praa Sands Golf Club,* Germoe Crossroads (0736 763445).

Rock, *St Enodoc Golf Club,* (020886 3216).

St Austell, *Carlyon Bay Hotel,* Carlyon Bay, 2¹/₂m E of St Austell (072681 4228).

St Austell Golf Club, Tregongeeves Lane, 1m SW of St Austell (0726 72649).

St Mellion, *St Mellion Golf & Country Club,* ½m NW of St Mellion (0579 50101).

Truro, *Truro Golf Club,* Treliske, 1½m W of Truro (0872 72640).

RIDING AND TREKKING

Bodmin, *The Lawrence Riding School and Stud Farm,* St Lawrence (0208 831223).

Davidstow, *Tall Trees Riding Stables* (08406 249).

Launceston, *Nine Tor Riding Centre,* North Hill (0566 232).

St Leonard's Equestrian Centre, Polson (0566 5543).

Liskeard, *Sunrising Riding Centre,* Henwood (0579 62895).

Looe, *Polypever Riding Stables,* Duloe (05036 3010).

Morwenstow, *Gooseham Barton Stables,* Gooseham (028883 204).

Newquay, *Trenance Riding Stables,* Trenance Lane (0637 872699).

St Austell, *Porth Hall Riding Centre,* Sticker (0726 74103).

Woodlands Riding Stables, Prideaux Road, St Blazey (072681 2963).

St Ives, *Old Mill Stables,* Lelant Downs (0736 753045).

Truro, *Chiverton Riding Centre,* Silverwell (0872 560471).

SAILING

See also **Watersports.**

Falmouth, *Flushing Sailing Club,* New Quay (0326 74043).

Mylor Yacht Club, Mylor Yacht Harbour (0326 74391).

Port Navas Yacht Club, near Constantine (0326 40419).

Restronguet Sailing Club, Mylor (0326 74536).

Royal Cornwall Yacht Club, Greenbank (0326 311105).

Fowey, *Fowey Gallants Sailing Club,* Amity Court (0326 832335).

Royal Fowey Yacht Club, Whitford Yard (0326 832245).

▲ The steep walkway leading down the cliffs at Tintagel

Helston, *Helford River Sailing Club,* Helford (032623 460).

Looe, *Looe Sailing Club,* Buller Street (05036 2559).

Marazion, *Mount's Bay Sailing Club,* Godolphin Steps (0736 710620).

Penzance, *Penzance Sailing Club,* Albert Pier (0736 64989).

St Austell, *Pentewan Sands Sailing Club,* The Harbour (0726 843849).

Porthpean Sailing Club, Porthpean (0726 66266).

St Mawes, *St Mawes Sailing Club,* Post Office (0326 270686).

Saltash, *Saltash Sailing Club,* Waterside Clubhouse (0752 845988).

Torpoint, *Torpoint Mosquito Sailing Club,* Marine Drive (0752 812508).

Wadebridge, *Rock Sailing Club,* The Quay, Rock (0208 2709).

WALKING

The Cornwall Coast Path runs 268 miles around the coast of Cornwall and provides spectacular walking. Inland are the much shorter Tinners' Way and the Saints' Way. See pages 35 and 36.

Country Parks afford safe, well-marked walking and many have nature trails.

For information about woodland walking, write to the Forestry Commission.

Walking in England's West Country is available free from the West Country Tourist Board, and tourist information centres will advise on local trails and urban walks.

WATERSPORTS

A variety of activities including sailing, water-skiing and windsurfing are available at the following centres. More information can be obtained from South West Water.

Falmouth, *Falmouth Windsurfing Centre,* Stithians Reservoir (0209 861083).

Padstow, *Padstow Boardsailing School* (0841 532383).

Portscatho, *Portscatho Windsurfing School* (0872 75342).

St Anthony, *Sailaway* (032623 357).

Widemouth Bay, *Outdoor Adventure* (028885 312).

USEFUL INFORMATION
ADDRESSES

English Heritage (EH), Bridge House, Clifton, Bristol BS8 4XA (0272 734472).

Forestry Commission, 231 Corstorphine Road, Edinburgh.

South West Water, Peninsula House, Rydon Lane, Exeter EX2 7HR (0392 219666).

The Cornwall Tourist Board, 59 Lemon Street, Truro TR1 2SY (0872 74057).

The National Trust (NT), Information Office, Lanhydrock, Bodmin PL30 4DE (0208 74281).

The West Country Tourist Board, Trinity Court, 37 Southernhay East, Exeter, Devon EX1 1QS (0392 76351).

FACT FILE

TOURIST INFORMATION CENTRES

Those marked with an asterisk are not open during the winter.

Bodmin, Shire House, Mount Folly Square (0208 6616).

Bude,* The Crescent Car Park (0288 4240/3576) and Stamford Hill, Stratton (0288 3781).

Camelford,* North Cornwall Museum, The Clease (0840 212954).

Falmouth, Town Hall, The Moor (0326 312300).

Fowey, 4 Custom House Hill (072683 3616).

Hayle, * Southern Cross Self-Serve, Loggans Moor (0736 754399)

Launceston, Market House Arcade, Market Street (0566 2321).

Looe,* The Guildhall, Fore Street, East Looe (05036 2072).

Lostwithiel, Community Centre, Liddicoat Road (0208 872202).

Newquay, Cliff Road (0637 871345).

Penzance, Station Road (0736 62207).

St Ives, The Guildhall, Street-an-Pol (0736 796297).

Truro, Municipal Buildings, Boscawen Street (0872 74555) and Victoria*, A30, Roche (0726 890481).

Wadebridge, Town Hall (020881 3725).

▼ Dancers celebrating spring in Helston

THEATRES AND CINEMAS

There are theatres in Falmouth, Newquay, Padstow, Penzance and St Ives, and cinemas in Bude, Newquay, Padstow, Penzance and St Ives.

EVENTS AND CUSTOMS

Although the events shown in this section usually take place in the months under which they appear, the actual dates of many vary from year to year.

Numerous other events such as fêtes, county shows, flower festivals and horse shows also crop up regularly in the area.

Full details of exactly what is happening where can be obtained from tourist information centres or local newspapers.

FEBRUARY

Hurling the Silver Ball, St Ives (Monday after the first Sunday after 3rd February); Columb Major (Shrove Tuesday and the following Saturday week)
Two teams battle for a silver-coated wooden ball.

APRIL

Trevithick Day, Camborne (last Saturday)
Dancers lead a cavalcade of steam through streets.

MAY

'Obby 'Oss, Padstow (1st) *'Oss is led through the streets with an accordian band and a prancing 'teazer'.*

Furry Dance, Helston (8th)
Mummers, dancing, celebrations.

Great Cornwall Balloon Festival, Newquay (3rd-6th).

JUNE

Royal Cornwall Show, Wadebridge (6th-9th).

Feast Week, Mevagissey (last week)
Carnival parades, dancing, sports.

Three Spires Festival, Truro (two weeks) *Concerts, readings, fringe events.*

Skinners Bottom Folk Festival, Blackwater, near Truro (three days) *Folk music, stalls, children's events.*

JULY

The Knill Ceremony, St Ives (25th) *Held every five years. Last held 1991.*

International Air Day, Culdrose, near Helston (24th) *Helicopters, jet fighters, aerobatics.*

AUGUST

International Air Day, RAF St Mawgan, near Newquay (7th).

Marhamchurch Revels, Marhamchurch (Monday after 12th) *Procession, country dancing, amusements.*

Fosters Lager Surf Masters Championship, Fistral Beach, Newquay (week prior to the bank holiday) *Top surfers in action.*

Cornwall Folk Festival, Wadebridge (bank holiday weekend).

SEPTEMBER

Cornish Gorsedd, Venue varies (first Saturday) *Gathering of Cornish bards.*

OCTOBER

Lowender Perran Celtic Festival, Perranporth, *Celtic musicians and dancers gather.*

Atlas

▲ Willa Park Head, Boscastle

The following pages contain a legend, key map and atlas of Cornwall, three motor tours and sixteen Cornish coast and countryside walks.

MAP SYMBOLS

THE GRID SYSTEM

The map references used in this book are based on the Ordnance Survey National Grid, correct to within 1000 metres. They comprise two letters and four figures, and are preceded by the atlas page number.

Thus the reference for Bodmin appears **92 SX 0767**

92 is the atlas page number

SX identifies the major (100km) grid square concerned (see diag)

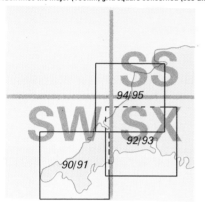

0767 locates the lower left-hand corner of the kilometre grid square in which Bodmin appears.

Take the first figure of the reference 0, this refers to the numbered grid running along the bottom of the page. Having found this line, the second figure 7, tells you the distance to move in tenths to the right of this line. A vertical line through this point is the first half of the reference.

The third figure 6, refers to the numbered grid lines on the right hand side of the page, finally the fourth figure 7, indicates the distance to move in tenths above this line. A horizontal line drawn through this point to intersect with the first line gives the precise location of the places in question.

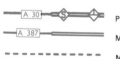

KEY MAP 1:500,000 - 1" TO 8 MILES ROAD INFORMATION

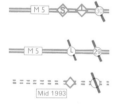

Motorway with service area, service area (limited access) and junction with junction number

Motorway junction with limited interchange

Motorway, service area and junction under construction with proposed opening date

Primary routes } Single and dual carriageway with service area

Main Road }

Main Road under construction

Narrow Road with passing places

other roads { B roads (majority numbered) / Unclassified (selected)

Gradient (1 in 7 and steeper) and toll

Primary routes and main roads

Motorways

Mileages are shown on the map between large markers and between small markers in large and small type.

1 mile = 1·61 kilometres

Motorways

A similar situation occurs with motorway routes where numbers and mileages, shown in blue on these maps correspond to the blue background of motorway road signs.

Primary Routes

These form a national network of recommended through routes which complement the motorway system. Selected places of major traffic importance are known as Primary Route Destinations and are shown on these maps thus  TRURO . This relates to the directions on road signs which on Primary Routes have a green background. To travel on a Primary Route, follow the direction to the next Primary Destination shown on the green backed road signs. On these maps Primary Route road numbers and mileages are shown in green.

WATER FEATURES

 } By Sea { Internal ferry route / External ferry route

Ferry .... Short ferry routes for vehicles are annotated Ferry

———————— Canal

Coastline, river and lake

GENERAL FEATURES

———————— Railway

AA..:A RAC..:R PO..:T Telephone call box

+-+-+-+-+-+-+-+-+ National Boundary

-------------------- County or Region Boundary

○ Large Town Town / Village

⊕ .... Airport

427. Height (metres)

TOURS

2 🚗	Start point of tour
—➤	Direction of tour
———	Featured tour
⑥	Point of Interest

TOURIST INFORMATION

⋏	Camp Site
⊞	Caravan Site
ℹ	Information Centre
P	Parking Facilities
☼	Viewpoint
⋈	Picnic site
⚑	Golf course or links
⛫	Castle
🕳	Cave
☗	Country park
✽	Garden
⊞	Historic house
⬥	Nature reserve
☆	Other tourist feature
🚂	Preserved railway
🏇	Racecourse
⋔	Wildlife park
🖾	Museum
✍	Nature or forest trail
ℼ	Ancient monument
✆	Telephones : public or motoring organisations
PC	Public Convenience
▲	Youth Hostel

ATLAS 1:208,545–1" TO 3¼ MILES
TOURS 1:250,000 – ¼" TO 1 MILE
ROADS AND RAILWAYS

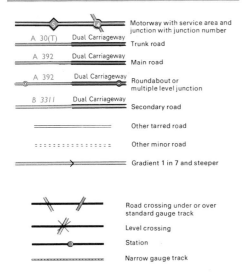

Motorway with service area and junction with junction number

A 30(T)   Dual Carriageway — Trunk road

A 392   Dual Carriageway — Main road

A 392   Dual Carriageway — Roundabout or multiple level junction

B 3311   Dual Carriageway — Secondary road

Other tarred road

Other minor road

Gradient 1 in 7 and steeper

Road crossing under or over standard gauge track

Level crossing

Station

Narrow gauge track

WATER FEATURES

Cliff
Slopes
Short ferry routes for vehicles
Flat rock
Transport for vehicles
Lake
Bridge   Ferry
Low water mark
Canal   Dunes   High water mark

GENERAL FEATURES

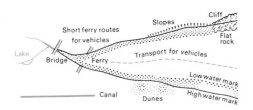

Buildings

Wood

Civil aerodrome (with custom facilities)

Radio or TV mast

Lighthouse

Telephones : public or motoring organisations

ANTIQUITIES

⁙ Native fortress

------ Roman road (course of)

Castle · Other antiquities

CANOVIVM · Roman antiquity

RELIEF

Feet	Metres	
		.274 Heights in feet above mean sea level
3000	914	
2000	610	
1400	427	
1000	305	Contours at 200 ft intervals
600	183	
200	61	
0	0	To convert feet to metres multiply by 0.3048

WALKS

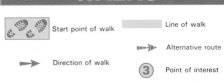

Start point of walk   Line of walk

Alternative route

Direction of walk

③ Point of interest

WALKS 1:25,000 – 2½" TO 1 MILE
ROADS, RAILWAYS AND PATHS

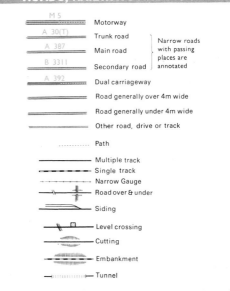

M 5 — Motorway

A 30(T) — Trunk road

A 387 — Main road ⎫ Narrow roads with passing places are annotated

B 3311 — Secondary road

A 392 — Dual carriageway

Road generally over 4m wide

Road generally under 4m wide

Other road, drive or track

Path

Multiple track

Single track

Narrow Gauge

Road over & under

Siding

Level crossing

Cutting

Embankment

Tunnel

GENERAL FEATURES

Church { with tower
or   { with spire
Chapel { without tower or spire

Gravel pit

Sand pit

Chalk pit, clay pit or quarry

Refuse or slag heap

Electricity transmission line

pylon pole

NT National Trust always open

NT National Trust opening restricted

FC Forestry Commission pedestrians only (observe local signs)

National Park

HEIGHTS AND ROCK FEATURES

Contours are at various metres / feet vertical intervals

50 · Determined { ground survey
285 · by   { air survey

Surface heights are to the nearest metre / foot above mean sea level. Heights shown close to a triangulation pillar refer to the station height at ground level and not necessarily to the summit.

Vertical Face

75
60
50
Loose rock   Boulders   Outcrop   Scree

PUBLIC RIGHTS OF WAY

Public rights of way shown in this guide may not be evident on the ground

--------- Public Paths { Footpath
— — — —   { Bridleway

+++++++ By-way open to all traffic

-+-+-+- Road used as a public path

Public rights of way indicated have been derived from Definitive Maps as amended by later enactments or instruments held by Ordnance Survey between 1 February 1968 and 1st November 1985 and are shown subject to the limitations imposed by the scale of mapping Later information may be obtained from the appropriate County Council.
The representation on this map of any other road, track or path is no evidence of the existence of a right of access.

Key to Atlas pages

Distances in miles to BODMIN
Map Ref: 92 SX 0767

Barnstaple	64	London	236
Bournemouth	148	Oxford	218
Bristol	146	Penzance	46
Cardiff	185	Plymouth	31
Exeter	60	Southampton	180

CORNWALL

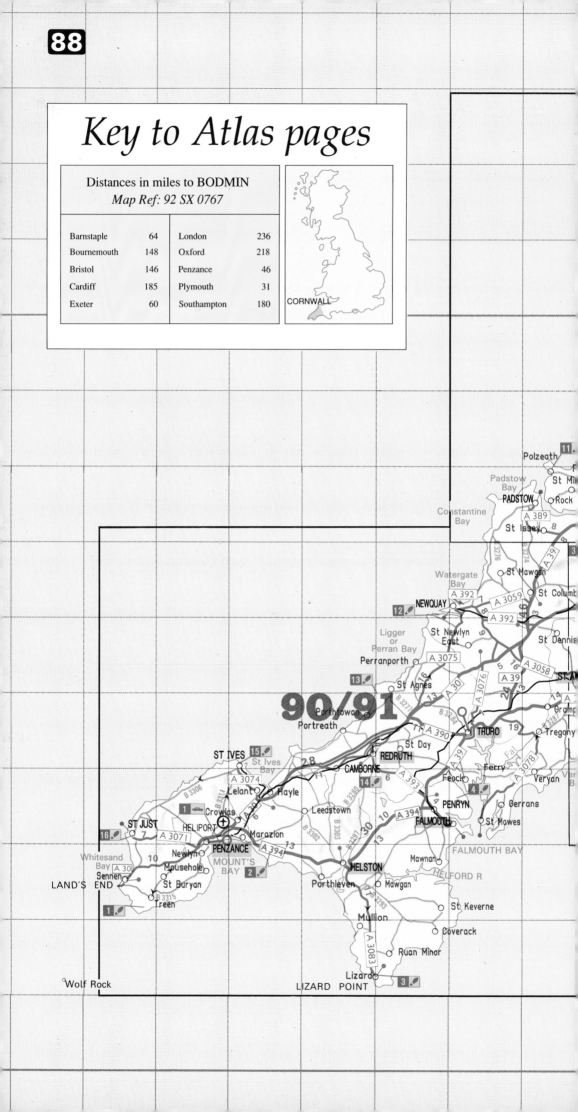

Polzeath **11**

Padstow Bay · St M

PADSTOW · Rock

Constantine Bay

A 389

St Issey · 8

3

St Mawgan

Watergate Bay

12 **NEWQUAY**

A 392 · A 3059 · St Columb

St Newlyn East · St Dennis

Ligger or Perran Bay

A 3075

Perranporth

5 · 16 · A 3058 · ST-A

A 39

13 St Agnes

A 30 · A 3076

Porthtowan

Portreath

A 390

St Day

90/91

A 39 · Grampe

TRURO · 19 · Tregony

ST IVES **15**

St Ives Bay

28

REDRUTH

CAMBORNE

A 393 · 6

Feock · Veryan

A 3074

Lelant · Hayle

14

Leedstown

A 394

PENRYN

FALMOUTH · St Mawes

Gerrans

A 3078

1 · Crowlas

HELIPORT

Marazion

ST JUST · 7

A 3071

16

Newlyn

PENZANCE

A 394 · 13

10 · Mawnan

FALMOUTH BAY

Whitesand Bay

A 30

10

Mousehole

MOUNT'S BAY

2

Sennen

HELSTON

HELFORD R

Newlyn · St Buryan

LAND'S END

Porthleven · Mawgan

St Keverne

1

Treen

B 3315

Mullion

Coverack

A 3083

Ruan Minor

Wolf Rock

Lizard · **3**

LIZARD POINT

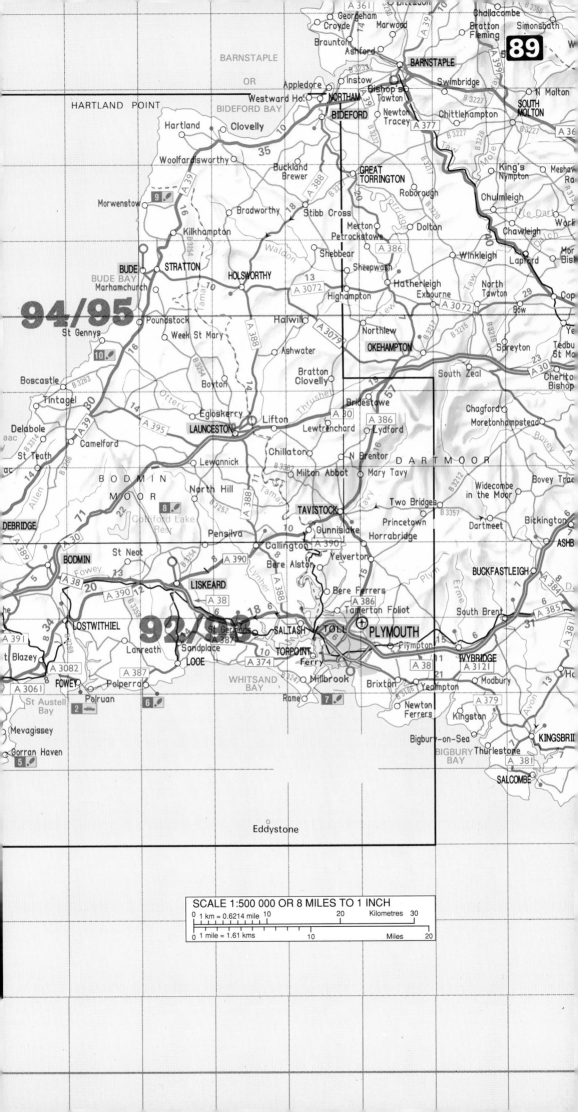

Kilometres 0   5   10

Miles 0   5

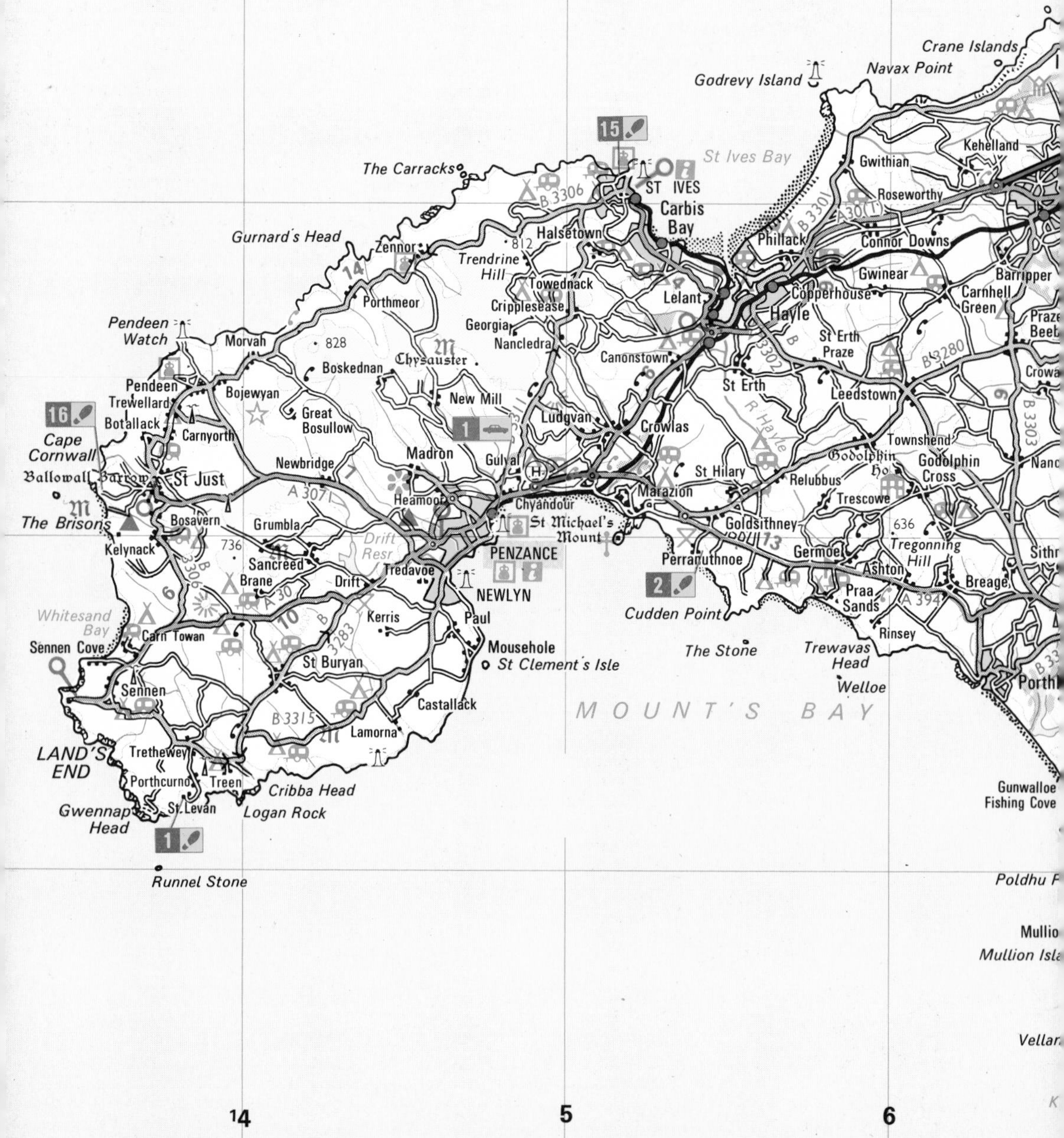

Crane Islands

Godrevy Island   Navax Point

St Ives Bay

The Carracks   Kehelland

ST IVES   Gwithian

Carbis Bay   Roseworthy

Gurnard's Head   Halsetown   Phillack   Connor Downs

Zennor   Trendrine Hill   Gwinear

Porthmeor   Towednack   Lelant   Copperhouse   Barripper

Pendeen Watch   Cripplesease   Hayle   Carnhell Green

Morvah   Georgia   Nancledra   St Erth   Praze

Pendeen   Boskednan   Chysauster   Canonstown   Crow

Trewellard   Bojewyan   New Mill   St Erth   Leedstown

Botallack   Great Bosullow   Ludgvan   Townshend

Cape Cornwall   Carnyorth   Newbridge   Madron   Crowlas   Godolphin Ho   Godolphin Cross

Ballowall   Gulval   St Hilary   Relubbus   Trescowe

The Brisons   St Just   Heamoor   Chyandour   Marazion   Nanc

Kelynack   Bosavern   Grumbla   St Michael's Mount   Goldsithney   Germoe   Tregonning Hill   Sithr

Sancreed   Drift Resr   PENZANCE   Perranuthnoe   Ashton   Breage

Brane   Drift   Tredavoe   NEWLYN   Cudden Point   Praa Sands   Rinsey

Whitesand Bay   Kerris   Paul   The Stone   Trewavas Head

Sennen Cove   Carn Towan   St Buryan   Mousehole   St Clement's Isle   Welloe   Porth

Sennen   Castallack   MOUNT'S BAY

Lamorna   Gunwalloe Fishing Cove

LAND'S END   Trethewey   Treen   Cribba Head

Porthcurno   Poldhu

Gwennap Head   St Levan   Logan Rock   Mullion   Mullion Isl

Runnel Stone   Vellan

Cambea

Fire Beacon Point

Boscastle

B 3263

Trevalga

Castle

Tintagel Head

Bossiney

Tintagel

B 3266

1009

Treknow

Trewarmett

Start Point

Treligga

Delabole

Camel

11

Helstone

St Teath

Port Isaac Bay

Rumps Point

11

Port Quin Bay

Port Isaac

B 3314

Cregeare Rounds

727

Pentire Point

Portquin

Portgaverne

11

New Polzeath

Trelights

Pendoggett

Michaelstow

Gulland Rock

Padstow Bay

Polzeath

St Endellion

527

Trebetherick

Trelill

St Breward

Tredrizzick

St Minver

Gunver Head

Crugmeer

Row

Trevose Head

St Kew

Quies

243

Rock

St Kew Highway

St Tudy

Chapel Amble

Constantine Bay

Trevone

257

435

Blisland

Trevarnon

PADSTOW

3

Bodieve

De

St Mabyn

St Merryn

Trevanson

B 3266

Shop

A 389

Little Petherick

WADEBRIDGE

Helland

Porthcothan Bay

8

Egloshayle

1

B 3276

St Issey

St Breock

20

Park Head

91

Penrose

9

Tredinnick

Burlawn

92

Bedruthan Steps

St Eval

Rumford

St Ervan

Washaway

Cardinham

St Breock Downs

BODMIN

14

TOUR 1

LAND'S END PENINSULA

Starting at Penzance, the drive visits the fishing villages of Newlyn and Mousehole, then veers inland and continues to Land's End. The coastal road to St Ives passes through rugged moorland interspersed with farms. Beyond St Ives Bay a detour is made to view St Michael's Mount.

ROUTE DIRECTIONS

The drive starts from Penzance ① .
46 Miles

Follow signs to Newlyn and Mousehole on an unclassified road along Penzance Promenade ② .

At Newlyn cross a bridge and turn left on to an unclassified road to Mousehole ③ .

Turn left down a very narrow lane to the harbour, then turn right and right again into Fore Street, signed Paul. Go up a steep hill past the church, signed Land's End. In just over ¹/₂ mile, turn left on to the B3315. Continue through Sheffield and in 1³/₄ miles pass the turning to Lamorna Cove.

Remain on the B3315 for 3¹/₄ miles. At the T-junction, turn left, signed Land's End. The road descends steeply, with a hairpin bend, then goes up to Treen ④ .

Continue on the B3315 for ³/₄ mile, then turn left, unclassified, to Porthcurno. From Porthcurno rejoin the B3315 and continue westwards. In ¹/₃ mile turn right. After 2 miles, turn left on to the A30 and drive for about ¹/₂ mile to Land's End ⑤ .

Return along the A30, to reach Sennen. Leave Sennen on the A30. After 1³/₄ miles, turn left on to the B3306, signed St Just. After 3 miles turn left at the T-junction on to the A3071 and enter St Just ⑥ .

Continue on the St Ives road, B3306, to Pendeen and Morvah ⑦ .

Continue on the B3306 to Zennor and St Ives ⑧ .

Leave St Ives on the A3074, signed Hayle. Pass through Carbis Bay and continue into Lelant ⑨ .

At Lelant turn right and in ¹/₂ mile bear right at the mini-roundabout, signed Penzance. At the next roundabout, take the third exit on to the A30, signed Penzance, passing through Crowlas.

After a further mile, at the next roundabout, take the second exit on to an unclassified road, signed Marazion. At the T-junction turn left across a railway bridge ⑩.

Return from Marazion along the unclassified road, signed Penzance. Cross the railway bridge and keep left, signed Longrock. Join the A30, then in ³/₄ mile, at a big roundabout, exit first left for Penzance.

POINTS OF INTEREST

① The mild climate has drawn visitors to Penzance since Regency times – as several handsome buildings in the town testify. The attractive harbour with its National Lighthouse Centre, the Penlee Memorial Gardens and the delightful Chapel Street with its famous Egyptian House are just a few of the reasons for spending time here.

② Newlyn is a major UK fishing port. It became famous for its artist colony in the 19th century and the Newlyn-Orion Gallery stages exhibitions by leading artists. Painters still both live and work among the quaint old cottages and fish cellars of Newlyn.

③ Pronounced locally as 'Mouzell', Mousehole is a typical Cornish fishing village – narrow alleyways, flower-filled courtyards and handsome granite cottages crowding round a small harbour.

④ Treen village lies just inland from a fortified headland known as Treen Castle – owned by the National Trust. A relative of Oliver Goldsmith overturned the 66-ton Logan Rock, a rocking stone perched on top of the headland and reached by a footpath from Treen. He was made to replace it at his own expense.

⑤ On a fine day the Isles of Scilly are visible 28 miles away to the west of Land's End – England's most westerly mainland point. The Longships Lighthouse can be seen offshore. Land's End has extensive tourist attractions and facilities.

⑥ St Just was an important centre last century when the nearby tin and copper mines were in full production. Now all closed, the mines and their ruined buildings are an interesting element of the surrounding landscape. The church in this lovely old village has a wall painting, and inscribed stone of the 5th century, and the shaft of a 9th-century cross.

⑦ On the moors above the hamlet of Morvah are Chun Castle and Chun Quoit – an Iron Age stone fort and a Neolithic chamber tomb. The village itself lies on the edge of the Penwith moorland.

⑧ Zennor is famous for a mermaid carving on one of the church's bench-ends, and for an associated legend. Old houses and winding alleys cluster beneath the 120ft spire of the 15th-century church in St Ives and around the handsome harbour. Once a busy pilchard fishing port, St Ives became the haunt of artists in the 1880s and today there are numerous galleries selling works of art. St Ives remains popular for its beaches – Porthmeor for surfers, Porthminster for families.

⑨ Lelant, originally a port on the Hayle estuary, declined when the river silted up. Now the marshland – the Saltings – is a sanctuary for feeding birds.

⑩ St Michael's Mount, with its splendid castle and priory, was given to the National Trust by the 3rd Lord St Levan in 1954, and can be reached by boat from Marazion, or on foot along a cobbled causeway at low tide. Marazion itself is an attractive place with Georgian and Victorian houses.

12

TOUR 2
CLAY MOUNTAINS AND GRANITE MOORLAND

Starting at Fowey on Cornwall's lovely south coast the drive heads inland through the lunar landscape of the clay country north of St Austell. It then crosses Bodmin Moor's ancient granite landscape, passing the famous Jamaica Inn before turning south once more to follow the River Fowey.

ROUTE DIRECTIONS

The drive starts from Fowey ① .
75 Miles

Leave Fowey on the A3082 and in just over 1 mile take the first exit left at a roundabout, signed St Austell. Continue on the A3082 passing under a railway bridge at Polmear. Bear left at the next junction and go through a built-up area to pass beneath another railway bridge (12' 6" headroom). About 100yds further on turn left at the T-junction, signed St Austell. Follow the road through Par under two more railway bridges ② .

At the T-junction with the A390 turn left and continue past access roads to Carlyon Bay and Charlestown on the left ③ .

Continuing on the A390, a busy roundabout is reached. Take the third exit, signed Bodmin. Within a few yards turn right, signed Bodmin B3374. Continue uphill and just part Carluddon, at a small roundabout, turn left, signed Stenalees ④ .

In just over 1 mile turn right into Stannary Road, signed Bodmin A391. At the Bugle Inn crossroads a diversion left can be made to Roche Rock ⑤ .

From the Bugle Inn crossroads continue on the A391 and at the next big roundabout take the second exit, signed Bodmin ⑥ .

Regain the A30 from Bodmin and after 8 miles turn right on to an unclassified road, signed Colliford Lake. Continue past the lake and turn left at the next junction, signed Dozmary Pool. Follow the road round the eastern side of Colliford Lake to pass Dozmary Pool on the right. At Bolventor turn right on to the A30 at Jamaica Inn ⑦ .

Just past Jamaica Inn branch right on to an unclassified road, signed St Cleer. Continue for several miles to the Golitha Falls ⑧ .

A short distance beyond the Golitha Falls turn right at a crossroads, signed Doublebois and Dobwalls. Keep right at a junction until reaching Doublebois. Cross the A38 and take the B3360, signed St Austell. In ¾ mile turn right on to the A390 and continue to Lostwithiel ⑨ .

Leave Lostwithiel on the A390 up a steep hill (1-in-6) and after 1 mile turn left, signed Fowey B3269. At the next roundabout turn left on to the B3269, signed Bodinnick Ferry. At the bottom of a steep hill turn right, signed Central Car Park, and reach Fowey.

POINTS OF INTEREST

① Fowey, pronounced 'Foy' unless you seek the scorn of locals, is delightfully placed on the banks of the River Fowey where it enters the sea. The houses of this ancient seaport rise dramatically from the water and the town's narrow streets and alleyways are characteristically Cornish and intriguing. Across the river is the equally lovely Polruan, which can be reached by passenger ferry.

② The port of Par was specially built in 1840 on reclaimed land although the Luxulyan River on which it stands was once tidal as far as St Blazey, over 1 mile upriver, until silt from tin streaming choked the estuary. A major port, Par was noted for shipbuilding. Export of china clay sustained the port for many years.

③ Charlestown is another product of the Industrial Revolution. Its impressive harbour was excavated in the last years of the 18th century. The port was initially used for exporting copper. There is a Visitor Centre with fascinating exhibits including those of shipwrecks.

④ The St Austell clay country is unique in Britain in terms of industrial landscapes. China clay was first extracted in the area in the mid-18th century. Later expansion of the industry caused problems of disposal of waste and the high pyramids and mesas of white quartz sand evolved into the remarkable lunar landscape of today.

⑤ Roche Rock comprises impressive pinnacles of hard granite within the clay country landscape. Built into the highest (60ft) pinnacle is a 15th-century chapel and hermitage dedicated to St Michael. The hermitage was once occupied by St Gonand, a leper.

⑥ Bodmin is a town of ancient lineage, strategically situated at the crossroads of several land routes through Cornwall. Its fascinating history is well recorded in the town's museum.

⑦ Jamaica Inn, famed in Daphne Du Maurier's novel, still retains the atmosphere of its romantic 18th-century origins. There is a Museum of Curiosity and a Potters Museum alongside.

⑧ The Golitha Falls, where the River Fowey pours foaming white between wooded banks, is worth a visit. The area incorporating the falls is a National Nature Reserve and has waymarked walks.

⑨ Lostwithiel was once the seat of the Duchy of Cornwall Parliament. It is a pleasing mix of architectural styles – from the 13th-century Old Duchy Palace with its medieval arch, to the town's well preserved Georgian houses. The attractive ruins of the Norman Restormel Castle are close by. Rebuilt by Edmund, Earl of Cornwall, it has magnificent valley views.

20

TOUR 3
KING ARTHUR'S COUNTRY

This is a drive of contrasts, including Tintagel – rich in romance and legends, Boscastle – with its stern cliffs and picturesque harbour, the sweeping sands of Bude and historic inland villages.

ROUTE DIRECTIONS

The drive starts from Wadebridge ① .
79 Miles

Leave Wadebridge on the A39, following the signs to Bude. Cross the river bridge, then at the mini-roundabout turn left. In ¹/₂ mile, at the traffic signals, turn left on to the B3314, signed Port Isaac. In 1¹/₂ miles cross Trewornan Bridge over the River Amble. In 2 miles turn left, unclassified, signed Rock. In 1¹/₄ miles, at Pityme, go round a left bend and within yards turn right into Trewiston Lane, signed Trebetherick and Polzeath ② .

Continue through Trebetherick and descend steeply (1-in-5) to Polzeath ③ .

Leave Polzeath and ascend sharply (1-in-7). After 2 miles branch left, signed Port Isaac. In ¹/₂ mile turn left on to the B3314 for St Endellion ④ .

Leave St Endellion on the B3314 for 1 mile, then turn left on to the B3267 for Port Isaac ⑤ .

At Port Isaac turn right, unclassified, and descend to Portgaverne. Pass through the village and ascend (1-in-10). After 2¹/₄ miles turn left on to the B3314 to Delabole ⑥ .

Leave Delabole on the B3314 for 1³/₄ miles, then turn left, unclassified, signed Tintagel B3263. Join the B3263, and pass through Trewarmett to Tintagel ⑦ .

From the Wharncliffe Arms Hotel in Tintagel turn right, signed Boscastle. Go through Bossiney and descend (1-in-9) then ascend steeply (1-in-6). Two miles further on turn left, signed Bude B3263. Descend to Boscastle ⑧ .

Leave Boscastle on the Bude road, B3263, cross the river bridge, and ascend steeply (1-in-6). After 3¹/₂ miles turn left and immediately left again, unclassified, signed Crackington Haven. In 2¹/₂ miles descend steeply (1-in-5) into Crackington Haven ⑨ .

Continue through Crackington Haven and ascend steeply (1-in-6). After 3 miles reach Wainhouse Corner and turn left on to the A39, signed Bude. Continue past Treskinnick Cross and Poundstock, then ¹/₂ mile further turn left, unclassified, signed Widemouth. After ³/₄ mile follow the sweep of Widemouth Bay to Bude ⑩ .

Leave Bude following signs for Bideford (A39). Shortly turn right, signed Camelford, A39. After 1 mile turn right on to the A39, signed Wadebridge, then turn left, unclassified, signed Marhamchurch. At Marhamchurch turn left, signed Week St Mary, then bear right. At Week St Mary turn right, signed Canworthy Water, and at the end of the village branch right, signed Canworthy Water. In 3¹/₂ miles, at the T-junction, turn left, signed Canworthy Water. Just over 1 mile further, turn right, signed Launceston, and cross the river bridge to Canworthy Water. Continue through Warbstow to Hallworthy. At Hallworthy turn right on to the A395, signed Wadebridge. In 2³/₄ miles turn left on to the A39, signed Wadebridge, to reach Camelford ⑪ .

Leave Camelford on the A39, passing St Kew Highway on the right to re-enter Wadebridge.

POINTS OF INTEREST

① Wadebridge claims the longest bridge in Cornwall, built by wealthy wool merchants in the 15th century. Today the town serves a wide agricultural area; the Royal Cornwall Show is held here annually.

② From Pityme a detour can be made to Porthilly via Rock, where the church of St Michael was dug from drifting sand. Rock is linked to Padstow by passenger ferry across the River Camel.

③ The main attractions at Polzeath are safe bathing and some of the best surfing in Cornwall. The tiny 13th-century church of St Enodoc was excavated from the sand in 1863 and restored. Sir John Betjeman is buried there.

④ Standing by the road at St Endellion is the lovely little church of St Endellienta. Inside are several quaint bell-ringers' rhymes, and a beautifully preserved tomb-chest.

⑤ Narrow alleyways known as 'drangs' wind between Port Isaac's slate cottages. The harbour has been a haven for fishing boats since before the Middle Ages. An inshore lifeboat is stationed here.

⑥ The Delabole region has been famous for its slate for nearly 600 years, and at the 500ft-deep Delabole Slate Quarry there is a museum and viewing area.

⑦ Linked by many writers with King Arthur, 12th-century Tintagel Castle has traces of a Celtic settlement, identified as the trading port of a chieftain's stronghold. The Old Post Office in the village high street – now in the care of the National Trust – is a 14th-century manor house. Nearby King Arthur's Hall was built in 1933 and contains an exhibition on Arthurian legends.

⑧ The village of Boscastle has a spectacular harbour entrance. In the past sailing ships were towed in by boats manned by oarsmen. The National Trust owns most of the land around the harbour.

⑨ At Crackington Haven a gorse-clad valley owned by the National Trust opens out on to a sandy beach. Surf is good here, but it can be dangerous.

⑩ Strong winds that have caused hundreds of wrecks over the centuries provide a constant supply of rollers at Bude, ideal for surfing. The town, developed as a family resort in Victorian and Edwardian times, was once linked by canal to Launceston.

⑪ One tradition places King Arthur's Camelot at Camelford. Slaughterbridge, which crosses the Camel River north of the town, is one of the contenders for his last battleground. The North Cornwall Museum is situated at Camelford.

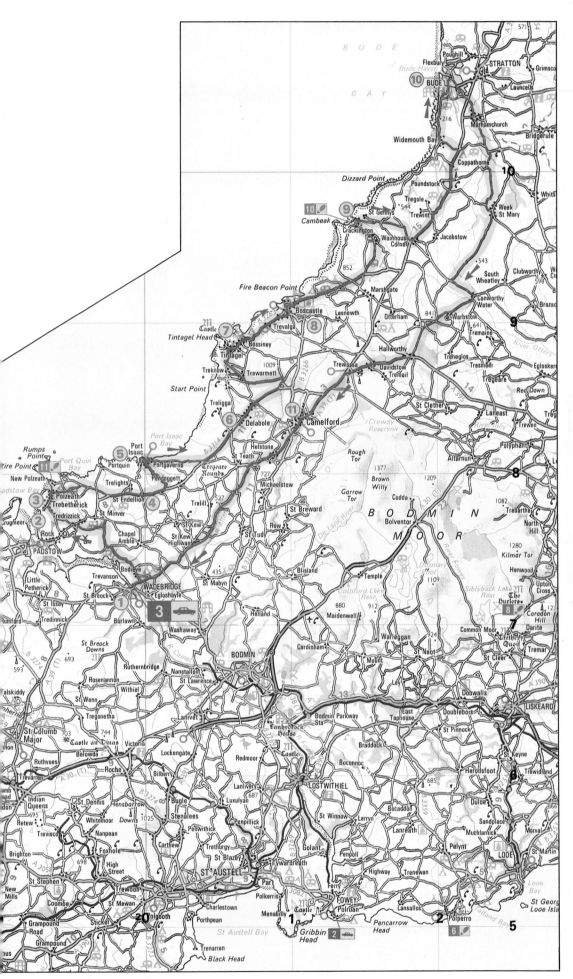

WALK 1

THE OTHER LAND'S END

From the little granite church of St Levan, the walk follows an ancient field track before joining the coast path above the spectacular cliffs at Gwennap Head, the 'Fisherman's Land's End'.

ROUTE DIRECTIONS

3 miles. Allow 2 hours
Start from the field above St Levan's Church, where you can park (grid ref. SW381222).

Walk to the road end, ignoring the beach path on the left ①.

Turn left at the road end and walk uphill past a cottage. A narrow path leads to a granite stile into a field, whose left edge is followed for 50yds to another stile. Cross this stile and go up the right edge of the field to another stile. Cross this and follow the left side of two fields to stiles, then cross three fields to stiles, all the time aiming north-west for a single house and farm buildings. Follow the left side of another field to a stile and a road that leads south past Lower Roskestal Farm.

After about ¾ mile, where the road bends sharply left, take the second obvious track on the right. This leads downhill across a stream, and up to the coastguard road. Follow the road round to the left for a few yards then take the track on the right up to the coastguard look-out at Gwennap Head ②.

Turn left in front of the look-out and follow the coast path to Porthgwarra Cove ③.

Go past the café/shop at Porthgwarra and turn right at the signpost. Then go left, uphill, and pass a house before turning right along the cliff-top. Keep right at the next junction until reaching St Levan's holy well ④.

Go down the rocky path towards the beach then continue along the top of the cliff to the next headland of Pedn-mên-an-mere ⑤.

Follow the path to the theatre car park. Follow the track from the car park to the road, then turn left and return to St Levan's Church.

POINTS OF INTEREST

① St Levan, a genial eccentric, was one of a number of Celtic saints who settled in Cornwall in the 6th century.

The present church has a remarkable font in the Norman style and in the churchyard there is a large granite rock, split in two, known as St Levan's Stone.

② The cliffs around Gwennap Head rise magnificently above the sparkling Atlantic. A mile offshore lies the Runnel Stone Buoy, marking the end of a notorious reef.

③ There is a beautiful little beach at Porthgwarra flanked by granite bluffs, with caves and tunnels carved from the rock. They were once used for access to the beach by horse and cart to collect seaweed for use as fertiliser.

④ St Levan's holy well, said to cure eye troubles, stands next to a roofless baptistry above Porth Chapel beach.

⑤ On the far edge of Pedn-mên-an-mere headland is the open-air Minack Theatre which has been carved out of the cliff to resemble a classical amphitheatre.

▼ St Levan's holy well above Porth Chapel beach

▲ St Michael's Mount rising like a fairytale castle from the sea

WALK 2

THE SMUGGLERS' ROYAL COAST

The eastern corner of Mount's Bay is famous for its views of the magnificent offshore island of St Michael's Mount. It also harbours Prussia Cove, a 19th-century base for a notorious but likeable smuggling family whose leader dubbed himself the 'King of Prussia'.

ROUTE DIRECTIONS

3¾ miles. Allow 3 hours
Start from the car park above the beach at Perranuthnoe (grid ref. SW539295).

Walk south-east along the road that flanks the lower end of the car park ①.

Where the road curves up to the left follow the rough lane directly ahead for a few yards. Turn sharp left by a house and follow a broad track that winds uphill to Trebarvah Farm. Go through the farmyard and bear right between some outbuildings to a short lane leading off right (signpost at ground level). Cross a stile and walk along the field's edge, ignoring a stile in the wall on the left ②.

Cross a stile into another field. Walk round the field to

Trevean Farm. Turn left and then right at a road. Just round the bend, at a signpost, cross a stile into a field on the left. Walk right along the edge of the fields as far as the boundary hedge of Acton Castle ③.

Go up left to a stile. Follow the right edge of the next field to where a stile leads into a lane. Turn right and follow the lane past Trenalls House. Turn left down a lane by a car park. Keep right at the first junction. Just past a thatched cottage the track merges into a path. Keep right at a junction. The left branch leads down to the charming Bessy's Cove ④.

Continue above the western rim of the Cove past some old fishing huts. Follow the coast path above small rocky coves. Cross a steeper section of headland below a solitary house. Ahead lies Cudden Point ⑤.

Beyond Cudden Point the coast path is followed across stiles and along the bottom edge of fields. Keep to the path along the edge of the cliff until just before Perranuthnoe; the path turns inland through a small meadow to a track which rejoins the road to the car park.

POINTS OF INTEREST

① The Domesday Book records that the Manor of Uthno, which now comprises the modern parish of Perranuthnoe, had a population of '3 slaves, 7 villagers and 8 smallholders'.

② The view across Mount's Bay from this point reveals St Michael's Mount in all its glory. Beyond lie Penzance and Mousehole on the far shores of the bay.

③ Acton Castle was built by Admiral John Stackhouse in 1775 as a base for his research into seaweeds. He produced a major work on the subject.

④ In the late 18th century Prussia Cove was the stronghold of a famous smuggler John Carter who called himself the 'King of Prussia' after Frederick the Great. The Carters kept their own battery of guns on the promontory to the east of Bessy's Cove.

⑤ Cudden Point may have been used as a look-out point and defensive 'cliff castle' during the Iron Age (1500BC–AD500).

WALK 3

LIZARD, LION AND LIFEBOAT

The Lizard is the most southerly point in Britain and although flat and bare inland, the coastal cliffs are dramatic and the sea always impressive. The walk takes in the famous lighthouse, and passes by the Lizard lifeboat-house.

ROUTE DIRECTIONS

4 miles. Allow 3 hours
Start at Lizard town where there is ample parking (grid ref. SW703126).

There are public toilets on the western side of the large village green. Take the road that leads north-west past the toilets and on to a rough track. Where the track ends by a house follow the footpath which leads down to the sea at Caerthillian Cove ①.

At the Cove go left. Follow the coast path round a series of headlands towards Lizard Point (the old Lizard Head). From here there are views across Mount's Bay to the far west of Cornwall. Go down into Pistol Ogo Cove. Cross a wooden bridge beneath the tamarisk trees of Pistil Meadow ②.

Continue to the modern Lizard Point, taking care as the path is sometimes close to the cliff edge, and crossing where there are cafés and souvenir shops. Pass in front of 'The Most Southerly House' in Britain and go up past the lighthouse ③.

Follow the path through the blackthorn groves above Housel Cove keeping right at the junction. Continue to Pen Olver Head and Bass Point where there is a coastguard lookout ④.

Keep to the signposted path to Hot Point and on to Kilcobben Cove. Go down the steps at the side of the lifeboat station and follow the coast path to Church Cove. Take the lane inland past thatched cottages and the church of Landewednack ⑤.

Follow the road back to Lizard town keeping left at main junctions.

POINTS OF INTEREST

① The Lizard area is noted for an abundance of wild flowers. The many rare and alien species include the tamarisk, a salt-resistant Mediterranean shrub. The cliffs at the Lizard itself are smothered with the exotic Hottentot Fig.

② *Ogo* is the Cornish word for cave. The name 'pistol' is associated with the wreck of the *Royal Anne* in 1720 when crates of firearms were washed ashore with the dead. However, the name is more likely to come from the Celtic word *pystil* meaning waterfall.

③ There has been a warning light on the Lizard since 1752. The modern light is the most powerful in the UK and is visible for 21 miles on clear nights. Its twin foghorns rise menacingly above the path. The offshore rock pinnacle is called Bumble Rock.

④ From Bass Point there is a good view across Housel Bay to the Lion's Den, a vast circular chasm in the cliff-top formed by the collapse of a sea cave in 1847.

⑤ The private houses at Landewednack Cove were once part of a pilchard processing complex. The 14th-century church of St Winwallo at Landewednack is the most southerly church in England and in 1678 the last sermon in the Cornish language was preached here.

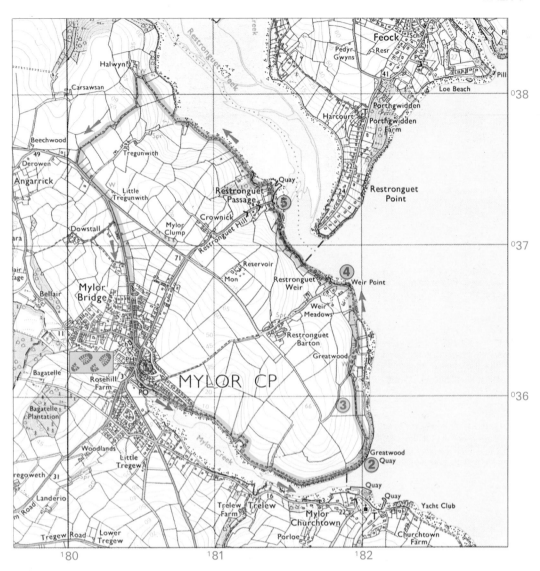

A FEW MILES ROUND MYLOR

This lovely walk reveals coastal Cornwall in a different light from that of rugged headland or sandy bay. The wooded country of Mylor is flanked on three sides by tidal creeks. There is a pleasant riverside pub midway.

ROUTE DIRECTIONS

4½ miles. Allow 3 hours
Start from the small car park at Mylor Bridge (grid ref. SW804363) just before the bridge.

The walk starts at Trevellan Road just across the road from the car park. Walk along Trevellan Road and go past signposts for Greatwood and Restronguet ①.

Where the road bends up to the left take the path directly ahead, in front of houses. The path turns left up a narrow alleyway to a road end. Turn right along a short stretch of path and go through a gate into a field. Continue through a number of fields along the creek, passing an old quarry and crossing a small causeway before reaching Greatwood Quay. Short sections of the path are often muddy in wet weather ②.

Continue along the track ③, from Greatwood Quay.

On reaching a junction with a narrow road turn right then left by the gates of Greatwood House. The well-signposted path leads to Restronguet Weir ④.

Cross the beach or use the permitted path at high tide. Continue to Restronguet Passage ⑤.

From Restronguet Passage follow the signposted track along the shore. The public right of way is clearly marked. Just past Restronguet Yacht Basin keep to the right along the shore. After about ½ mile the track curves inland and climbs through fields to Halwyn. Bear left at the junction of lanes by Halwyn and follow the farm track to the public road. Go left, keep right at the junction and continue down Bells Hill to the car park.

POINTS OF INTEREST

① The River Fal diverges into a number of creeks, each one a quiet sheltered anchorage stolen from the sea.
② Greatwood Quay is an ancient landing-stage. Directly opposite is Mylor Yacht Harbour once a famous Naval dockyard. Post Office sailing ships were also serviced here during the 'packet' service era up to the mid-19th century. Across the broad sweep of Carrick Roads lies the lovely Roseland Peninsula.
③ One of the delights of this walk in spring and summer is the luxuriance of wild flowers growing on either side of the path, where daffodils and primroses give way to bluebells and others.
④ The path from Greatwood to Restronguet Weir runs parallel with Carrick Roads, the third largest natural harbour in the world. The main channel is very deep and it is not uncommon to see massive sea-going vessels sticking out from behind headlands.
⑤ Restronguet Passage was on the route of the old Post Road from Falmouth to Truro. There was a rowing-boat ferry link with Feock for at least 500 years. The Pandora Inn could not be more conveniently placed for walkers and waterfolk.

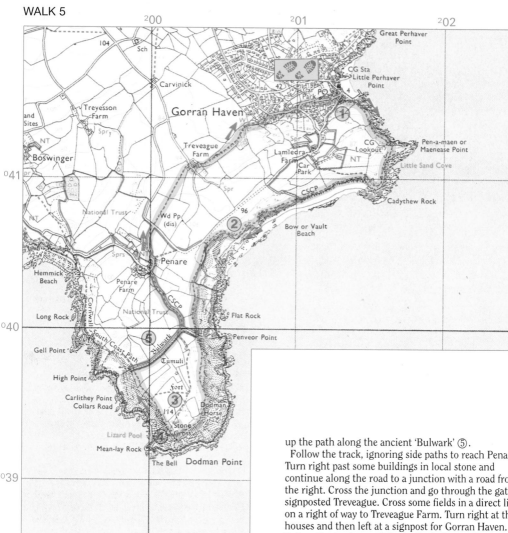

up the path along the ancient 'Bulwark' ⑤.

Follow the track, ignoring side paths to reach Penare. Turn right past some buildings in local stone and continue along the road to a junction with a road from the right. Cross the junction and go through the gate signposted Treveague. Cross some fields in a direct line on a right of way to Treveague Farm. Turn right at the houses and then left at a signpost for Gorran Haven. Follow the track round the back of a house. Go through a gate into a field on the left, signposted Gorran Haven. Follow a track downhill then go right across often wet ground to a lane between houses. Turn right at the road and walk back to the car park.

WALK 5

HAVEN AND CROSS

Dodman Point, known locally as 'Deadman' lies south-west of Gorran Haven. The Point still retains the features of Iron Age ditch and rampart fortifications.

ROUTE DIRECTIONS

4¼ miles. Allow 3 hours
There is a good car park at Gorran Haven (grid ref. SX011415).

From the car park walk down towards the harbour and beach. Turn right at Foxhole Lane, signposted Vault Beach ①.

Continue along the coast path keeping right just past a stone bench. The path leads up steeply past a memorial plaque. There is an easier alternative along the lower path round Maenease Point. At Vault Beach follow the path right and uphill ②.

Cross a wooden stile at a welcome seat. Continue to Dodman Point keeping left along the top of sloping fields then through a small wood. Continue left of more fields, cross a wooden stile on the left and continue to the cross on Dodman Point ③.

From the cross return to the junction of the paths and go directly across for a few yards ④.

Go back to the junction and turn right at the signpost to follow the path above Veryan Bay. Cross a wooden stile and turn sharp right by a gate, signposted Penare. Walk

POINTS OF INTEREST

① Gorran Haven, a tiny remote village which rivalled Mevagissey in the heyday of pilchard fishing, has had seven quays since the 13th century. The present quay was built in 1885 and has been repaired frequently. There is a delightful 15th-century chapel of ease above the beach, probably sacred for many centuries before the present church was built. Built on the rocks the chapel has an unusual tower, with five sides, and altar rails of old timber. In one of the windows there are three sea pictures, one with this church and cottages in the background. Although surrounded by modern houses, the heart of Gorran retains its traditional complex of buildings and narrow lanes with names like Rattle Alley.

② Vault Beach has a wide access track which was probably once used by farmers for carting the seaweed away from the beach and up to their fields where they used it as fertiliser.

③ The rather stark looking cross on the summit of The Dodman was erected as a navigational aid to mariners in 1896 by 'Parson' Martin the rector of St Michael Caerhays. The Dodman itself is a superb feature composed of hard sedimentary rocks that have resisted weathering. It is now in the care of the National Trust.

④ This short diversion along the opposite path leads to the Dodman Watchhouse; used in the late 18th century as one of a chain of Admiralty signal stations.

⑤ The Dodman was a magnificent Iron Age promontory fort. The surviving earthworks, 'The Bulwark', is massive and the defensive bank and ditch runs for 2,000 feet across the shoulders of the headland. Dense scrub patches on this headland attract a variety of migrant birds and are also heavily used by resident songbirds, as nesting sites.

▲ Polperro harbour, surrounded by some simple Georgian houses

WALK 6

POLPERRO AND TALLAND

Polperro is the epitome of Cornish fishing villages, with the sea literally outside its front windows. To the east lies Talland Bay with its delightful 13th-century church.

ROUTE DIRECTIONS

3½ miles. Allow 2 hours to include a visit to Talland Church.
Start from the car park at Crumplehorn just outside Polperro (grid ref. SW205515).

Walk down the hill into Polperro passing the old Crumplehorn Mill with its restored wheel ①.

Continue to Polperro Harbour ②.
At the inner end of the harbour go left across the Roman Bridge and past the House on Props to turn right into The Warren. Go along above the harbour and out along the cliff edge. At a junction take the lower path, by a National Trust sign, and pass above a tiny light beacon ③.
At a T-junction turn right and keep right at the next junction, signed Talland. Continue past the strikingly situated war memorial at Downend Point ④.
Continue to a road by a private house. Turn right and follow the road to where it bends up to the left. On the bend take the path that leads off directly ahead. At a T-junction with a track go right and follow the road that skirts Talland Beach ⑤.
Follow the road up to Talland Church ⑥.
From the church retrace your steps to the junction of the coast path and the steep track leading uphill. Go up the steep track to join a lane which is followed keeping straight ahead at a T-junction. Continue past some houses on the left where the lane widens then narrows and goes steeply downhill. Turn left at a junction with another lane and go down the very steep Talland Hill into Polperro ⑦.

POINTS OF INTEREST

① This centuries-old mill site has been renovated in recent years. Farmers used to toss silver coins on to the revolving wheel for good luck and good harvests.
② Polperro Harbour is steeped in sea history and has a colourful past that included every sea-going trade including smuggling. It retains its marvellous architectural integrity and a small, though thriving, fishing industry.
③ The tiny light beacon at Spy House Point exhibits a flashing white light at night visible for eight miles.
④ The stretch of coast from Downend Point to Talland Bay was bequeathed to the National Trust in 1948 by Angela Brazil, the popular writer of school stories for girls who lived at Polperro.
⑤ This lonely coast was famous for smuggling in past centuries. Even modern smugglers attempted unsuccessfully to land drugs at Talland Bay in the 1980s.
⑥ The 13th-century Talland Church with its unusual detached tower and slate gravestones flanking the approach path, has a magnificent collection of carved bench-ends. Note the stocks in the porch.
⑦ The seemingly endless and very steep Talland Hill is a fine example of how settlements in busy Cornish coves expanded and adjusted to difficult terrain with a delightful mix of housing.

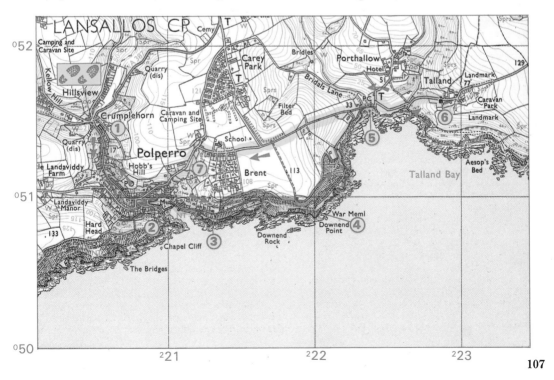

WALK 7
RAME HEAD RAMBLE

A circular walk on the Rame Peninsula with fine views across Plymouth Sound to the Devon shore and along the eastern sweep of Whitsand Bay into Cornwall.

ROUTE DIRECTIONS

4¾ miles. Allow 2½ hours
Start from the large car park above Cawsand (grid ref. SX432503). Cawsand can be reached either from the A38 or by the Plymouth to Torpoint ferry.

From the car park go down the road into Cawsand ①.
 Just before the village square turn right into Pier Lane by a coast path sign. Keep to the lower track along The Earl's Drive before climbing to Penlee Point ②.
 From Penlee Point follow the metalled track to where it curves sharply back to the right. Cross a stile directly ahead on to the coast path and follow this to Rame Head where a path leads out to the 14th-century St Michael's Chapel ③.
 Rejoin the path and turn sharp left by a footpath sign, keeping parallel with a stone wall up on the right. Continue across Queener Point with the great sweep of Whitsand Bay on the left ④.
 Go left at a signpost above a tennis court. The path leads steeply down some stone steps. Cross a track by the gate of a house. Go down more steps and through a gate to reach another track. Turn right and follow the track uphill to the road ⑤.
 Cross the road and go down the road opposite for about 120yds. Just before some buildings go left into a field by a signpost. (Alternatively the road can be followed downhill to Cawsand). Go the length of the field keeping the hedge on your right. At the bottom of the hill, at a gap, turn

right and go down over wet ground to a stile into a lane. Turn right then left on to the road to Cawsand.

POINTS OF INTEREST

① Cawsand and Kingsand are linked villages once divided by the ancient Cornwall–Devon boundary. Both are now wholeheartedly Cornish and are worth exploring for their delightful period atmosphere.
② The Earl's Drive was built by an Earl of Mount Edgecumbe in the early 19th century. The Earl also built the strange 'grotto' at Penlee Point. It is called Adelaide's Chapel and was built in honour of Princess Adelaide, wife of Prince William the future King William IV.
③ The headland was once an Iron Age fortification protected by a deep ditch which is still visible. Rame Head has also been used as a chapel, hermitage and a light beacon for shipping.
④ On the shore below the path is the privately owned Polhawn Fort, part of the defensive ring of costly forts built round Plymouth in the 1860s when fears of a French invasion were rife.
⑤ The road that runs above Whitsand Bay linked other forts and batteries and is still shown on some maps as a Military Road. It remained closed until the 1930s.

▼ The broad, sandy expanse of Whitsand Bay

WALK 8
THE WATER MARGIN

The south-eastern corner of Bodmin Moor is a charming landscape of wooded valleys, lakes and rivers, still punctuated here and there by the gnarled and rocky summits of moorland hills.

ROUTE DIRECTIONS

3½ miles. Allow 2½ hours to include a visit to Golitha Falls.
Start from the large car park at the roadside on the eastern side of Siblyback Lake (grid ref. SW237706). There is also parking within the lakeside reception area. In wet weather sections of the route can be muddy.

From the car park walk left for a few yards and gain the lakeside path via a wooden gate on the right. Continue to the dam ①.

From the dam take the path signposted Trekeivesteps and go left on to the access road to the lower dam. Reach the public road at Trekeivesteps. Turn left for Draynes Bridge and the entrance path to Golitha Falls ②.

Retrace your steps back up the road from Draynes Bridge for a short distance to a footpath sign by a gate, on the right opposite a row of houses. Go through the gate on to rough open ground. An indistinct path winds through the marshy ground diagonally leftwards in line with some trees on a raised bank. Keep the trees to the left and turn right at a junction with a more distinct path. Keep right where the path divides. Continue through a small oak wood by the stream ③.

Cross a stile by a signpost. Go straight ahead and through a gate. Follow a muddy track round to the left. Just before some buildings veer right over a stream at a signpost to reach a road. Turn left and pass South Trekeive Farm. Just past the farm turn left up a rough lane. Bear sharp left at a field gate and follow the lane between low walls ④.

Where the lane ends, go through a gate into a field. Continue past a solitary tree, bearing slightly left to reach a rocky area of ground ⑤.

Continue gently downhill and through a gate to reach Siblyback Dam. Return along the lakeside to the car park.

POINTS OF INTEREST

① Siblyback Lake Reservoir was opened in 1969. It has a maximum capacity of 700 million gallons. It is a top class trout fishery and a busy water sports centre in the summer.

② The Golitha Falls are unusual for Cornwall where there are few big rivers. The falls, impressive after prolonged rain, were even more magnificent many years ago when there was a high triple fall. It was blasted in an effort to create a salmon passage which failed.

③ The remains of past industrial use have subtly changed the landscape alongside the stream. It is likely that mineral processing was involved. The trench running along the banks of the stream may have been a water leat.

④ The lane from South Trekeive is a fine example of the old 'green' roads that once connected farm hamlets and villages; they are sunk into the landscape rather than imposed on it.

⑤ Even amidst green fields the underlying bones of this granite country break through. Skeletal walls indicate that this area may well have been the site of ancient settlements.

WALK 9
HAWKER'S MORWENSTOW

The northern corner of Cornwall is a remote and lovely place where the land runs deep and green to the very edge of the cliffs; a fitting place for the remarkable Victorian, Robert Stephen Hawker, poet, cleric and engaging eccentric.

ROUTE DIRECTIONS

3½ miles. Allow 3 hours
Start from the car park above Morwenstow Church (grid ref. SS205153).

A visit to the church is recommended ①.

From the car park follow the path towards the coast and go left at the coast path. The cliff edge is quite sudden in places and great care should be taken. Make the short detour to visit Hawker's Hut, signposted ②.

Continue along the path and descend steeply into the valley of Tidna Shute. Cross the stream and two wooden stiles. Climb steeply to Higher Sharpnose Point and pass the old coastguard lookout ③.

Continue along the coast path, crossing several wooden stiles. The huge satellite communication dishes at Cleave Camp Satellite Station can be seen ahead. Go down the steep slope to Stanbury Mouth then take the track leading inland with the stream on your right. Stay on the track until it reaches a metalled road. At Stanbury Farm look out for a stile in the left-hand wall opposite the farm buildings. Cross the stile and follow the right of way across the field to a stile in the opposite wall. Continue across the next field and through a gate to Tonacombe ④.

Take the muddy track running off diagonally left from the main farm track behind the house, then cross a stile into a small field. Go through the gate opposite and follow the right-hand edge of the next field to reach the Tidna Stream ⑤.

Cross the stream and follow the path to the rear of the Bush Inn. Go down the left side of the Inn and through a gate on to the road. Turn left for Morwenstow.

POINTS OF INTEREST

① Morwenstow Church has magnificent Norman carvings on its porch and a splendid interior. The privately owned vicarage below the church has five chimneys designed by Parson Hawker. They represent the towers of three Cornish churches, a college tower at Oxford and the tombstone of Hawker's mother.

▼ The magnificent, verdant cliff-top path near Morwenstow

② The Rev'd Robert Stephen Hawker (1803–1875) was incumbent at Morwenstow from 1834 to 1874. He has been the victim of myth and sensationalism, but was still extraordinary. Hawker retrieved the bodies of many drowned sailors and gave them Christian burials in the churchyard. Each had his own grave, but there are no headstones or other marks. Hawker dressed in seaman's jersey and boots and spent many hours meditating in his hut, smoking opium and writing poems including the famous ballad *The Song of the Western Men*. He was also responsible for re-creating the pagan harvest festivals in a Christian form.

③ From Higher Sharpnose there are splendid views north to Vicarage Cliff with its 'comb' of shaly rock known as 'culm', thrusting seawards; a coastal feature that repeats itself all the way to Bude and beyond.

④ Tonacombe is a Tudor manor house of the 15th century. It has striking gateposts and several courtyards and would have been the centre of an extensive estate. Within are contemporary wooden panellings and vast open hearths, and a minstrels' gallery.

⑤ The Tidna is a typical feature of the North Cornish coast where streams cut deep valleys in the soft culm measures. In spring and summer the wooded banks host a profusion of wild flowers.

WALK 10

THE STRANGLES

A spectacular cliffside walk south from Crackington Haven matched by a return trip along a deeply wooded valley captures the remarkable contrasts of the coast of North Cornwall.

ROUTE DIRECTIONS

4 miles. Allow 3 hours
Start from the car park at Crackington Haven (grid ref. SW143970).

Take the coast path west from Crackington Haven ①.

The path leads out to a point above the distinctive promontory of Cambeak. **Approach to the tip of the promontory along the crumbling ridge is not recommended for walkers** ②.

Continue along the coast path for about 1 mile and pass some distinctive quarried workings on the inland side of the path above The Strangles beach ③.

Go up left to an open field past a signpost. Go diagonally right across the field to a stile in its far right-hand corner. This leads on to a road. Turn left then immediately right over a stile into a field. Bear right across the field and down into a stream bottom below Pengold Farm. Cross the stream bottom and go uphill to a signpost. Continue at a slight angle in front of the farm buildings to a signpost on a bank. Go left at an angle from the bank to another signpost by a gate ④.

Go through the gate, turn right then immediate left and walk along the top edge of a steeply inclined field. Continue in a direct line following signposts into the bottom of the wooded valley below Trevigue Farm ⑤.

Take the track signposted Crackington Haven and follow a delightful path keeping to the valley bottom all the way. When houses come into view ahead, cross the stream by a footbridge. Turn left at the T-junction. Cross another stream and continue to a farm. Go along the track through the farmyard to Crackington Haven.

POINTS OF INTEREST

① Crackington Haven was used in the past as a landing point for lime and coal for a local limekiln. Slate was exported from local quarries.

② This stretch of the Cornish coast has a complex geological history and has leant its name to a rock type known as the Crackington Measures. These are typified at Cambeak with its spectacular zig-zag folds.

③ Donkeys were once used to collect sand and slate from The Strangles beach. A new path now leads down to the beach where the novelist Thomas Hardy once went courting from St Juliot vicarage near Boscastle with his future wife Emma.

④ The careful signposting in this area, where a definitive right of way exists but is not obvious, is a tribute to the cooperative spirit among farmers, landowners and the local authorities.

⑤ Trevigue is a 16th-century farmhouse, although altered through time and renovated in the late 18th century. It is now in the care of the National Trust and offers cream teas during the summer. It can be reached by diverting uphill from this point in the walk.

WALK 11
ABOVE DOOM BAR

Pentire Point and Rumps Point lie on the eastern side of Padstow Bay. Both headlands dominate this dramatic stretch of coastline, with the great cliff faces of Pentire best viewed from Rumps Point.

ROUTE DIRECTIONS

3½ miles. Allow 2½ hours
Start from the main entrance of the car park at New Polzeath (grid ref. SW936795).

Turn right and then right again into Gulland Road. At the end of this road, where it joins Baby Beach Lane, take the coast path opposite. Go round the small cove of Pentireglaze Haven, continue to junction with path going off right to Pentire Glaze Farm. Stay on the lower coast path to Pentire Point ①.

▼ Pentire Point and the off-lying Newland Rock, from Polzeath

From Pentire Point continue along the coast path until reaching the path that leads on to the Rumps headland. Follow this path on to the head ②.

Return to the main path and continue with the wall on your right ③.

Where the coast path turns sharply left at the junction of two walls, go right over a stile and head for a line of tamarisk shrubs ④.

At the shrubs turn left. On reaching Pentire Farm, go straight through the yard. Abreast of the farmhouse, go through a gateway on the right into a lane (muddy in wet weather). This becomes a path leading downhill to the coast path above Padstow Bay, where a left turn up some wooden steps leads back to New Polzeath.

POINTS OF INTEREST

① The views across Padstow Bay from Pentire Point are magnificent. In fine conditions, the Camel Estuary appears to be a calm, secure waterway but it is marred by the suitably named Doom Bar – a dangerous ridge of sand and silt that has built up between the headlands. Yet Padstow, which lies on the west bank of the River Camel, was a busy port in years past and is still a flourishing fishing harbour.

② The Rumps, with their remarkable pinnacles, are composed of greenstone, whereas the rest of Pentire is pillow lava that erupted from ancient volcanoes. From the Rumps the vast main wall of Pentire is visible.

③ Looking back to the Rumps, it is obvious why the promontory made an ideal cliff castle. Three Iron Age earth ramparts with ditches were constructed across the saddle.

④ Tamarisk grows well in these coastal areas. In July and August its graceful, slender branches are covered in rosy-pink, scented flowers.

WALK 12
SAND COUNTRY

The great headlands south of Newquay enclose large areas of golden sand within charming coves like Porth Joke and wide sweeping expanses like Crantock Beach. Inland lie The Kelseys, an area of open grazing that merges with the sand dunes of Holywell Bay.

ROUTE DIRECTIONS

4¼ miles. Allow 3 hours
Start from the car park at West Pentire Village (grid ref. SW776606).

Go down the road from the car park entrance and turn left. Go through the gate signposted West Pentire Head and continue along the track, ignoring a footpath going off left to Polly Joke. A few yards further on turn right at a gate and join the coast path bearing left above Crantock Beach ①.

Continue to Pentire Point West keeping to the seaward path and skirting the cliff edge with care in places until reaching the lovely little cove of Porth Joke ②.

Cross the head of the cove and follow the coast path to Kelsey Head ③.

Continue round Kelsey Head and along the edge of Holywell Bay to a gate at the beginning of the sand dunes. Follow a wooden boardwalk through the dunes and then up the beach to Holywell. Keep to the boardwalk section through the dunes ④.

Just before the car park and café/shop at Holywell village turn sharply left in front of a row of bungalows. Keep to the sandy path that winds up through the dunes and skirts a golf course. Go through a gate on to the wide expanse of The Kelseys ⑤.

Where the Golf Course ends, go through a gate on the right. Turn sharp left and when the wire fence veers off left carry straight on to reach a track leading down from the isolated house known as The Common. Go left all the way to the valley bottom. Where the track bends back inland cross a stile on the left and go along by a wall. Cross the stream and turn left at the track that leads steeply uphill to the car park.

POINTS OF INTEREST

① The River Gannel reaches the sea at the northern end of Crantock Beach. The river mouth is now heavily silted but cargo ships once came nearly ¾ of a mile up river. It was once the natural port for Newquay and a landfall on the Ireland–Brittany route. In ancient times travellers embarked and disembarked here to travel across Cornwall on foot en route for Brittany, thus avoiding sailing round the treacherous Land's End.

② The charming Porth Joke seems ill-named, but Joke is simply a corruption of a Cornish word *gwic* meaning creek while 'porth' means harbour or cove. Alternative meanings suggest Chough's Cove or Flower Haven.

③ Kelsey Head was once the site of an Iron Age cliff castle. All that remains are signs of a bank and ditch fortification.

④ The sands of Holywell are very mobile and the National Trust, who own the main area of The Kelseys, is carrying out extensive planting with marram grass which binds the shifting sand. Legend claims that an ancient city lies beneath the offshore sand between Newquay and Perranporth. Walkers are requested to keep to the boardwalk paths through this part of the dunes.

⑤ In spring and summer the duneland supports many unique plants and wild flowers including the attractive sea holly with its sea-blue leaves.

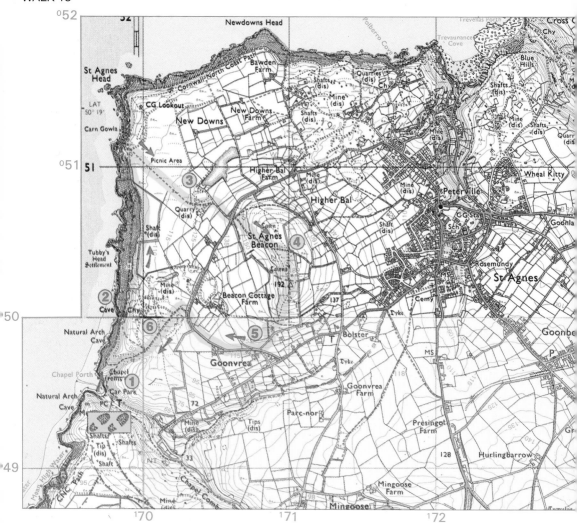

WALK 13
ST AGNES BEACON

The shapely hill of the Beacon rises above the old mining village of St Agnes. South of St Agnes lies the small cove of Chapel Porth. Between lies a dramatic coast rich in the remains of a once vigorous mining industry.

ROUTE DIRECTIONS

3¼ miles. Allow 2½ hours
Start from the car park at Chapel Porth (grid ref. SW697496).

Walk north from Chapel Porth on the coastal path keeping to the broadest track up a small valley ①.

Where the track branches, keep left and continue to the splendid mine stack remains at Towanroath ②.

Continue along the coast path ignoring side paths to right and left. Keep to the path; the slopes to seaward are steep. The path turns steeply uphill. At a junction with a broad track turn left and reach a bench just before the beginning of a metalled road. Turn sharp right at the bench and follow a right of way inland, keeping the wedge-shaped remains of a building directly ahead. Ignore paths veering off to the left. The path runs alongside a field with concrete-post fencing and then merges with a metalled road ③.

Follow the road and at a T-junction turn right to reach a junction with the main road. Cross to a National Trust sign. Take the right-hand track to the top of St Agnes Beacon ④.

Follow the track leading down the south side of the Beacon. Where the slope eases go right for a few yards then turn sharp left down a path by a mine shaft warning post ⑤.

Turn right at a track and right again at the main road. After ⅓ mile turn left at a National Trust sign for Wheal Coates. Go down a broad track and take the path leading off left ⑥.

Bear left past a bench and continue on the downhill path to Chapel Porth.

POINTS OF INTEREST

① Grass and thrift-covered mounds are all that remain of the medieval St Agnes Chapel which once stood halfway up the small valley; hence the name Chapel Porth.
② The striking ruin of the Towanroath engine house has been well preserved by the National Trust. The building dates from 1872 and housed a pumping engine to keep the Wheal Coates mine dry. Water would be sucked up by the rise and fall of the steam piston that led down the shaft now covered with an iron grid.
③ This area would have been a hive of industrial activity throughout the 18th and 19th centuries. There are large deposits of clay and sand left from the ancient geological eras when the surrounding land was below sea-level. The sand was used in glass making. Quarrying is still carried out.
④ St Agnes Beacon is 629ft high and commands outstanding views across Cornwall in clear weather. Bonfires have traditionally been lit from the earliest times to celebrate battles won, and events of great note.
⑤ The area of St Agnes Beacon and the coastal shelf is riddled with mines and their open shafts. Many have been capped using a steel mesh cone. Some of these cones are visible but others are indistinct. It is unwise to venture off marked paths.
⑥ The ruined buildings over to the right were the processing works of the Wheal Coates mine.

WALK 14

CARN BREA – THE GIANT'S HILL

The distinctive rock-studded hill of Carn Brea with its quaint castle and rather stern monument rises dramatically above the urban landscape of Camborne and Redruth. Carn Brea was the home of a mythical giant. The hill lies at the heartland of Cornwall's remarkable industrial past yet retains its rough moorland character.

ROUTE DIRECTIONS

2¼ miles. Allow 1½ hours
The summit ridge of Carn Brea is reached by a lane leading up from the village of Carnkie (grid ref. SW686399) which itself is best reached from Redruth. Cars can be taken to the top of the lane where there is informal parking.

Walk along the track and turn left to the monument ①.

Retrace your steps and go along the track to Carn Brea Castle ②.

Continue past the castle for a few yards to a point just beyond a leaning slab of rock. Turn sharp right and follow a narrow path downhill ③.

Stay on the main path in line with a church and graveyard on the flat ground below. Go down a final steep section of path and turn left at a broad track. At a junction with a track coming in from the right continue left for a few yards to where some large slabby boulders line the left edge of the track. Turn sharp left midway along the line of boulders and follow a path that leads uphill in line with the skyline midway between castle and memorial. Follow the track bearing left to pass an electricity pole ④.

Turn right where the path reaches a T-junction with another path running down from the top of the hill ⑤.

Follow the path downhill and go left along the base of the hill keeping left until abreast of a distinctive square-cut rock on the crest of Carn Brea. Continue up a steep rise on to a raised area and descend the other side to a junction of several paths. Take the path leading sharply left and uphill ⑥.

Bear right towards a stone wall. On the crest of the hill where paths cross, follow the path directly ahead. Continue along the path to where it joins the lane just below a house. Turn left and return to the car.

POINTS OF INTEREST

① Carn Brea is 828ft high. At the summit stands the 90ft Dunstanville Monument, striking in size but hardly elegant. It was built in 1837 in honour of a local nobleman. Note the large rock with scooped hollows east of the monument. The hollows were caused by rainfall erosion and were not man-made for Druidical blood sacrifices as Victorian writers feverishly claimed.
② The castle is Carn Brea's other monument and one that is more appealing and imaginative. Some form of castle built within the existing rocks has been here since the 15th century.
③ The slopes to the right of the path were part of a large Neolithic settlement over 5,000 years ago. It has been estimated that upwards of 150 people would have lived in thatched, wooden lean-to huts. Hundreds of flint arrow-heads have been found during excavations at Carn Brea.
④ Carn Brea has been popularised for generations as the home of giants. Many of the rock features on the hill are so named and include The Giant's Hand, Head, Cradle, Couch, etc. The scooped rock described in ① is known as the Giant's Cups and Saucers.
⑤ The mounds and hollows on the lower part of the hill are the remains of extensive tin-processing works.
⑥ The deep trench running off to the right was a quarry, the material of which would have been used for mine works.

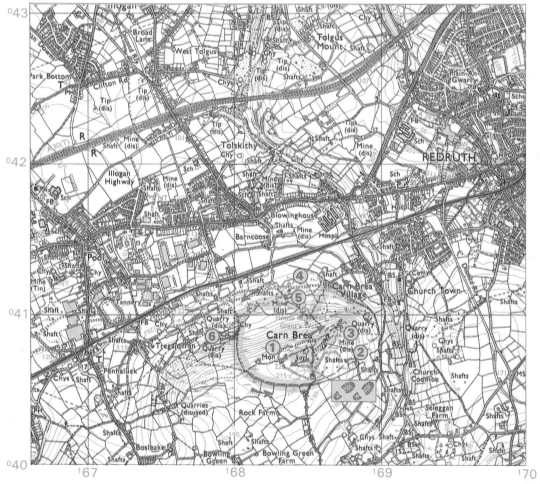

WALK 15
POINTS WEST FROM ST IVES

The coast west of St Ives has a number of 'Points' or headlands flanked by incut coves and steep-sided 'zawns', the spectacular sea-ravines which make the Cornish coast so remarkable. This walk follows the coast path to Clodgy Point and Hor Point where it turns inland and then leads back to St Ives along an ancient field path.

ROUTE DIRECTIONS

2¾ miles. Allow 2 hours
Start from the car park above Porthmeor Beach, St Ives (grid ref. SW515408).

Walk up past the toilets and turn right alongside the putting and bowling greens. A tarmac path leads to the rocky headland of Carrick Du known locally as Man's Head ①.
  Follow the coast path to the grassy slopes of Clodgy

▼ Looking across St Ives' harbour to the church of St Ia

Point. Skirt the edge of the low cliff and then head for the distinctive square-cut rock on the horizon ②.
  From the square-cut rock, walk uphill until reaching a low wall where the path goes through a gap. Follow the path round to the right to cross a boggy area well supplied with stepping stones. Continue for about ½ mile to where the main path bends sharply inland towards a substantial stone wall. Turn left on to a broad track which is followed inland for ½ mile to a point where field stiles lie to right and left ③.
  Cross the stile on the left and follow the left edge of small fields over several stiles marked with black and white posts ④.
  Beyond the last stile in the sequence, walk on for about 30yds towards a wooden signpost; then turn sharp left down a narrow area of field which merges into a path. A few yards down the path cross a stile on the right. Turn left down the field edge and cross a stile into a narrow, hedged-in path by the side of a house to reach a lane ⑤.
  Turn right and follow the lane to a T-junction with a road. Turn left here and follow the road downhill to where it turns sharp left down a steep hill towards the Porthmeor Beach car park.

POINTS OF INTEREST

① The Land's End Peninsula is famous for its golden granite, but many of its northern cliffs are made up of rocks called greenstone or *killas* (Cornish for 'clay'). Man's Head is a particularly striking example of a greenstone outcrop.
② Vast numbers of migrating birds pass close to headlands like Clodgy Point, especially in autumn when driven inshore by stormy weather. Kittiwakes numbering 20,000 per day have been recorded.
③ From here the shapely inland hills of West Penwith can be seen on the skyline. These are part of the high backbone of granite ridges running to Land's End in pleasing contrast to the sea.
④ The path crossing from right to left is an ancient field path linking St Ives to the village of Zennor.
⑤ The layout of this section of path is an example of how the encroachment of the modern world on established country ways may be sensibly resolved. The integrity of the right of way has been preserved with the minimum intrusion to neighbouring properties.

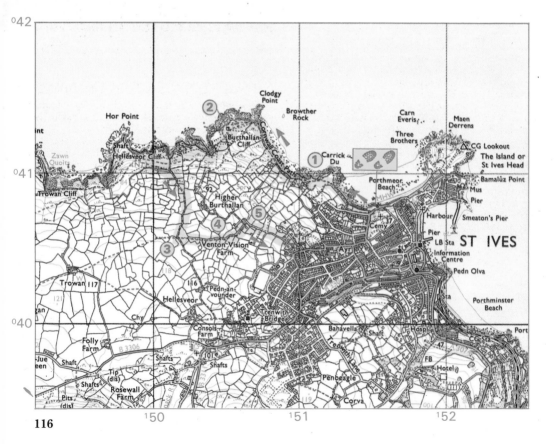

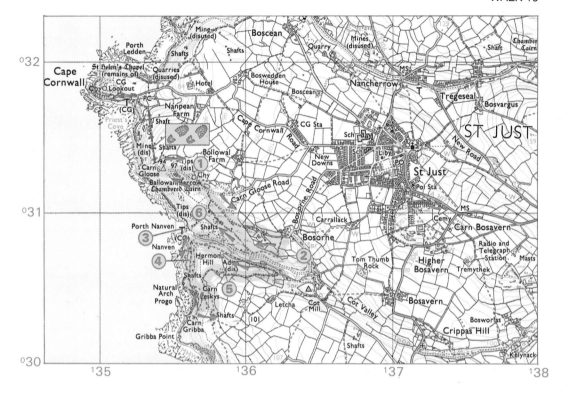

WALK 16

THE MINERS' PATH

West of Cape Cornwall lies the lovely Cot Valley running down to the Atlantic shore at Porth Nanven. The valley was once given over to mining and many signs of its industrial past remain although nature and its wild flowers have taken over.

ROUTE DIRECTIONS

3¼ miles. Allow 2 hours
Start from the road end at Carn Gloose (grid ref. SW354313) which is reached from St Just.

Walk back along the road to Ballowall Barrow ①.
Continue along the road and turn right on to a track 100yds beyond a handsome chimney stack. At a junction continue direct to reach a lane by some houses. Go along the lane for a short distance until abreast of some buildings on the left. Go through a gate on the right and follow the left-hand wall of the field to a stile which leads into a delightful walled path. Descend steeply and go down a stepped stile ②.
Turn right then left at a broad track to join the road. Turn right and walk down to the road end at Porth Nanven ③.
Cross the slab bridge over the valley stream and follow the coast path uphill. Continue past several open rifts in the hillside on the left. **These should not be entered** ④.
Follow the path to where it turns sharply uphill between boulders. Continue on the winding path to a T-junction with a path on the top of the cliff. Turn left here and follow the path inland to cross a handsome stile behind a house. Go down and turn left on to the path in front of the house and walk down towards the cove ⑤.
Just above the cove another path leads sharply down to the right between two pointed stones. Cross a plank bridge over the stream and turn right at the road. Just past an earthy cave in the bank on the left, an uphill path goes off left, then right to join a broad track. Turn left up the stony track and pass some fenced-off mine shafts ⑥.
Just beyond the last mine shaft, branch right and then left beyond the coast path sign. Turn left at the road for Carn Gloose.

▲ The Bronze Age cairn on the cliff-top at Carn Gloose

POINTS OF INTEREST

① Ballowall Barrow is a Middle-Late Bronze Age entrance grave dating from the period 1400–600BC. It was probably the traditional burial place of local chieftans.
② This section of a very ancient right of way was cleared in 1990 through the admirable efforts of a local man. It reflects how such practical 'heritage' can lie hidden from modern generations.
③ To the right of the cove at Porth Nanven is a startling example of a raised beach where the land has tilted up from sea-level in distant geological time. The cliff-face is studded with rounded sea boulders that would have once been part of a beach.
④ These dark passageways are old mine adits. They would have been either used for draining mine workings, or are the result of excavation of mineral lodes.
⑤ The network of paths throughout the area was used extensively by miners. Many of the paths were water leats originally cut for harnessing power for the mass of surface machinery used in mining.
⑥ The closeness of the mine shafts indicates just how intensive 19th-century mining was in the area. Hundreds of shafts were created around St Just, the deepest ones being sunk to over 2,000ft with tunnels running out beneath the sea. Cot Valley had some of the oldest mines in Cornwall.

ACKNOWLEDGEMENTS

The Automobile Association wishes to thank the following photographers, libraries and associations for their assistance in the preparation of this book.

R Bishop 36 St Petroc; *Cornish Life Magazine* 15 Flamank Plaque, 21 St Pirons Oratory, 37 Holywell Luxwan; *Cornwall Archaeological Unit* 7 St Dennis, 8 Zennor, 9 Restormel Castle; *Cornwall Garden Society* 29 Tregothnan, 30 Trewithen, 31 Trebah; *County Museum & Art Gallery, Truro* 8 Gold Collar, 10/1 Botallack Mine, 17 Pendennis Castle, 19 Jan Tregeagle, 55 Shipwreck; *Hulton* 22 Death of Arthur; *Mary Evans Picture Library* 18 The Giant Bolster, 39 D H Lawrence; *National Trust Cornwall Regional Office* 14 Sir Richard Carew, 28/9 Cotehele Valley Gardens, 31 Glendurgan; *Nature Photographers Ltd* 23 Rock Pool, Shore Crab, 24 Burnet Rose (A J Cleeve), 24 Fulmar, Waterspider, Puffin (P R Sterry), 25 Dog Whelk (A J Cleeve), 26 Yellow Flag (G Grey Wilson), 27 Marsh Orchid (A J Cleeve), Otter (W S Paton), Grey Seal (D A Smith); *Newlyn Orion* 59 Painting by Stanhope Forbes; *Rex Features* 56 Prince Charles; *Royal Institute of Cornwall* 74 Dolly Portreath; *G Sutton* 26 Green Hairstreak; *The Mansell Collection* 16/7 St Michael's Mount, 19 Giant Killer, 20 Mermaid, Little People; *World Pictures* (Cover) Polperro

All remaining pictures are held in the Association's own library (A A Photo Library) with contributions from: A W Besley, P Goodrum, A J Hopkins, B Johnson, A Lawson, S & O Mathews, N Ray, R Newton, T Teegan, W Voysey, H Williams.

Other Ordnance Survey Maps of Cornwall

How to get there with the Routemaster and Routeplanner Maps

Reach Cornwall from Cardiff, Bristol, Birmingham, London, Dover and Bournemouth using Routemaster map sheets 8 and 9.
Alternatively use the Ordnance Survey Great Britain Routeplanner which covers the whole country on one map sheet.

Exploring with Landranger and Touring Maps

Landranger Series
1¼ inches to one mile or 1 : 50 000 scale
These maps cover the whole of Britain and are good for local motoring and walking.
Each contains tourist information such as parking, picnic places, viewpoints and rights of way.
Sheets covering Cornwall are:
190 Bude and Clovelly
200 Newquay and Bodmin
201 Plymouth and Launceston
203 Lands End, The Lizard
204 Truro and Falmouth

Touring Map of Devon and Cornwall
This map, at a scale of 1 inch to 3 miles, will help you discover the whole of the beautiful West Country.
The map includes Tourist Information such as camping and caravan sites, country parks and sandy beaches.

Other titles available in this series are:

Brecon Beacons; Channel Islands; Cornwall; Cotswolds; Days out from London; Devon and Exmoor; East Anglia; Forest of Dean and Wye Valley; Ireland; Isle of Wight; Lake District; New Forest; Northumbria; North York Moors; Peak District; Scottish Highlands; Snowdonia; South Downs; Wessex; Yorkshire Dales